Fiona Mapp

ESSENTIALS

Year 7

KS3 Mathematics

Coursebook

How to Use this Coursebook

A Note to the Teacher

This is the first of three mathematics coursebooks for students at Key Stage 3.

Together, the coursebooks for Years 7, 8 and 9 provide full coverage of the programme of study for Key Stage 3 mathematics.

Each coursebook comprises...
- clear, concise content appropriate to that year
- questions and tasks to reinforce students' learning and help improve their confidence.

Where appropriate, the coursebooks relate mathematical concepts to real-life situations, to illustrate the importance of maths beyond the classroom.

This Year 7 coursebook is split into 18 topics. Each topic has the following features:
- **Content** that students need to learn.
- **Key words** picked out in colour in the text and listed at the end of the section.

- A **Quick Test** to assess students' understanding through a combination of theory-based questions, multiple choice questions and true/false questions.
- **Skills Practice** questions to provide students with the opportunity to practise what they have learned.

Selected topics have an **extension/activity** to further reinforce students' understanding. These take the form of a practical activity or investigation.

Also included in the centre of the book is a pull-out answer booklet. It contains the answers to all of the questions in this coursebook.

Each coursebook is supported by a workbook to provide further practice and help consolidate learning.

A Note to the Student

We're sure you'll enjoy using this coursebook, but follow these helpful hints to make the most of it:
- Try to write answers that require reasoning or explanation in good English, using correct punctuation and good sentence construction. Read what you have written to make sure it makes sense.
- Think carefully when drawing graphs. Always make sure that you have labelled your axes, given your graph a title and plotted points accurately.
- Try to learn what all the key words mean.

- Where questions require you to make calculations, remember to show your workings. In tests, you might get marks for a correct method even if you arrive at the wrong answer.
- The tick boxes on the Contents page let you track your progress: simply put a tick in the box next to each topic when you're confident that you know it.

You might need a calculator to answer questions that carry this symbol. All other questions should be attempted without using a calculator and you should show your workings.

Contents

Numbers

Place Value

Our number system was invented in India by mathematicians about 1400 years ago.

The value of a digit depends on its place in a number.

In this place value diagram, the digit 6 means...

1000 Thousands	100 Hundreds	10 Tens	1 Units	
2	7	1	⑥	6 units
Two thousand, seven hundred and sixteen				
8	3	⑥	5	6 tens
Eight thousand, three hundred and sixty-five				
3	⑥	2	2	6 hundreds
Three thousand, six hundred and twenty-two				
⑥	9	1	0	6 thousands
Six thousand, nine hundred and ten				

A place value diagram can help you to read large numbers:

10 000 Ten thousands	1000 Thousands	100 Hundreds	10 Tens	1 Units
7	5	6	3	9
Seventy-five thousand, six hundred and thirty-nine				

The largest UK National Lottery jackpot was £42 008 610, that's forty-two million, eight thousand, six hundred and ten pounds.

Ordering Large Numbers

When sorting large numbers, firstly sort them by the highest-value digits.

For example, 3-digit numbers should first be sorted by the hundreds digits, then the tens digits, and then the units.

Example

Put these numbers in order of size, smallest first:

719, 642, 711, 317, 306, 207, 159

Sort by the 100s digits.	159, 207, 317, 306, 642, 719, 711
Sort by the 10s digits.	159, 207, 306, 317, 642, 719, 711
Sort by the units.	159, 207, 306, 317, 642, 711, 719

Rounding to the Nearest Ten

To round a number to the nearest ten, look at the digit in the units column:
- If it is less than 5, round down
- If it is 5 or more, round up.

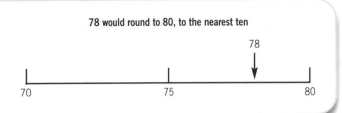

78 would round to 80, to the nearest ten

Rounding to the Nearest Hundred

Rounding a number to the nearest hundred is similar to rounding to the nearest ten, except you look at the digit in the tens column:
- If it is less than 5, round down
- If it is 5 or more, round up.

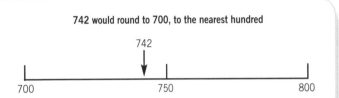

742 would round to 700, to the nearest hundred

Rounding to the Nearest Thousand

To round a number to the nearest thousand, look at the digit in the hundreds column:
- If it is less than 5, round down
- If it is 5 or more, round up.

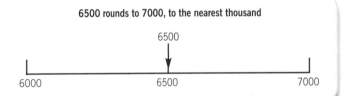

6500 rounds to 7000, to the nearest thousand

Estimating

Rounding numbers can help when estimating the answers to calculations.

Estimating can be useful when shopping so that you have a rough idea of how much your shopping bill should be.

It's also a good way of checking calculations.

When estimating...
- round the numbers to easy numbers, usually to the nearest ten, hundred or thousand
- use these easy numbers to work out the estimate
- when multiplying or dividing, never round a number to zero.

Examples
1. 9 + 21 is approximately 10 + 20 = 30
2. 12 × 402 is approximately 10 × 400 = 4000

Numbers

Addition

When adding numbers using a written method, it's important to line up the place values.

Example

Work out 276 + 5291

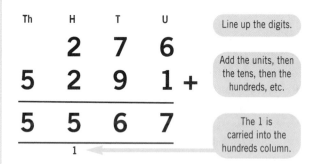

Line up the digits.

Add the units, then the tens, then the hundreds, etc.

The 1 is carried into the hundreds column.

This addition can be checked mentally by using **partitioning** and an empty number line:

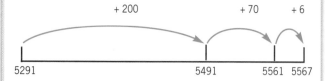

Estimating to check gives
300 + 5300 = 5600 approximately.

Market traders often calculate the costs of goods by mental methods.

Subtraction

When subtracting numbers, place values must line up one on top of the other. Subtracting is also known as 'finding the **difference**'.

Example

Work out 642 – 129

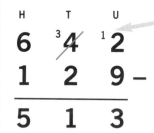

In the units column, 2 – 9 won't work. Borrow 10 from the next column, so the 4 becomes a 3 and the 2 becomes 12.

This subtraction can be checked by subtracting too much and then **compensating** by adding on the extra.

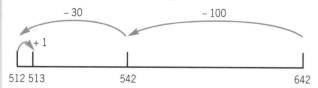

Quick Test

1. Write the following number in words: 9832
2. To sort large numbers in order of size, do you look at the digit with the highest place value or the lowest place value first?
3. Amy is told to round the number 636 to the nearest ten.
   a) What is the place value of the digit that she needs to work with?
   b) Should she round the digit up or down? Explain your answer.

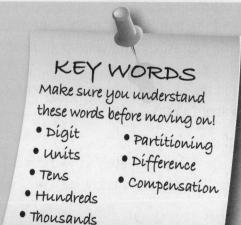

KEY WORDS

Make sure you understand these words before moving on!

- Digit
- Units
- Tens
- Hundreds
- Thousands
- Partitioning
- Difference
- Compensation

1 What does the 6 mean in each of these numbers?
  a) 629　　　**b)** 4276　　　**c)** 3006　　　**d)** 2651　　　**e)** 267

2 What does the 3 mean in each of these numbers?
  a) 3157　　　**b)** 2369　　　**c)** 52 032　　　**d)** 143　　　**e)** 49 385

3 Write the following numbers in digits:
  a) Four thousand, six hundred and thirty-eight.
  b) Six hundred and five thousand, two hundred and nine.
  c) Eighty-three thousand and thirty-nine.
  d) Nine thousand, seven hundred and five.
  e) Two hundred thousand and seventy-three.

4 Put these numbers in order of size, starting with the smallest:
  a) 62, 7, 93, 127, 156
  b) 201, 1169, 37, 58, 291
  c) 5, 37, 18, 26, 52, 41
  d) 583, 1271, 162, 837, 26

5 Round the following numbers to the nearest 10:
  a) 65　　　**b)** 71　　　**c)** 279　　　**d)** 1374

6 Round the following numbers to the nearest 100:
  a) 727　　　**b)** 1493　　　**c)** 6281　　　**d)** 3079

7 Round the following numbers to the nearest 1000:
  a) 5216　　　**b)** 12 931　　　**c)** 18 500　　　**d)** 79 657

8 Describe one method that can be used for estimating the answer to an addition.

9 Is the following subtraction set out correctly? Explain your answer.
  549
  23   –

10 Estimate the answers to these calculations:
  a) 33 + 28　　**b)** 615 + 893　　**c)** 76 – 18　　**d)** 1032 – 564

11 Charlie is in the supermarket and wants to buy the groceries on her list, but she only has £10. Estimate how much the shopping will come to. Does Charlie have enough money?

Shopping list

Jam tarts
White loaf　　　69p
Pizza　　　　　75p
Caster sugar　　89p
Bread roll　　　73p
Biscuits　　　　44p
Mushrooms　　　49p
Yoghurt　　　　31p
Yoghurt　　　　64p
Baking potatoes　64p
Rump steak　　　£1.34
　　　　　　　　£1.87

12 Work out...
  a) 529 + 14　　**c)** 8291 + 842　　**e)** 725 – 361
  b) 603 + 27　　**d)** 629 – 143　　**f)** 1752 – 169

13 The answer to an addition sum is 693. Give one example of what the question could be.

Multiplication and Division

Multiplication Tables

You need to know the multiplication tables up to 10×10.

For example, you can see from the table that:

$7 \times 4 = 28$
$4 \times 7 = 28$
$28 \div 7 = 4$
$28 \div 4 = 7$

×	1	2	3	4	5	6	7	8	9	10
1	1	2	3	4	5	6	7	8	9	10
2	2	4	6	8	10	12	14	16	18	20
3	3	6	9	12	15	18	21	24	27	30
4	4	8	12	16	20	24	28	32	36	40
5	5	10	15	20	25	30	35	40	45	50
6	6	12	18	24	30	36	42	48	54	60
7	7	14	21	28	35	42	49	56	63	70
8	8	16	24	32	40	48	56	64	72	80
9	9	18	27	36	45	54	63	72	81	90
10	10	20	30	40	50	60	70	80	90	100

Multiplying and Dividing by 10, 100 and 1000

When multiplying a number by 10, you move each digit one place to the left and put a zero on the end.

e.g. $72 \times 10 = 720$

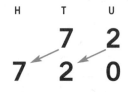

When multiplying a number by 100, you move each digit two places to the left and put two zeros on the end.

e.g. $63 \times 100 = 6300$

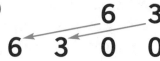

When multiplying a number by 1000, you move each digit three places to the left and put three zeros on the end.

e.g. $9 \times 1000 = 9000$

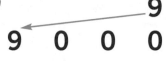

When dividing a number by 10, you move each digit one place to the right. If the original number ends in zero, it's lost from the end.

e.g. $750 \div 10 = 75$

Multiplying and Dividing by 10, 100 and 1000 (cont.)

A similar process applies when dividing a number by 100 or 1000.

Examples

1. $6300 \div 100 = 63$
2. $2700 \div 1000 = 2.7$

Multiplication

Multiplying two or more numbers together is called finding the **product**.

Multiplication is usually used to solve problems.

Example

A school shop orders 9 boxes of rulers.
Each box contains 25 rulers.
How many rulers did the school shop order?

$$
\begin{array}{r}
25 \\
9 \times \\
\hline
225 \\
\hline
{\scriptstyle 4}
\end{array}
$$

$9 \times 25 = 225$ rulers

Multiplying a 3-Digit Number by a 2-Digit Number

There are two different methods that you can use to multiply large numbers together:

* the grid method
* long multiplication.

Example

Sarah works in a stationary store.
She earns £272 per week.
How much does Sarah earn in a 52-week year?

Method 1 – the grid method:

×	200	70	2
50	10 000	3500	100
2	400	140	4

$$
\begin{array}{r}
13\,600 \quad {\scriptstyle 10\,000\,+\,3500\,+\,100} \\
544 + \quad {\scriptstyle 400\,+\,140\,+\,4} \\
\hline
14\,144 \\
{\scriptstyle 1}
\end{array}
$$

Method 2 – long multiplication:

$$
\begin{array}{r}
272 \\
52 \times \\
\hline
544 \quad {\scriptstyle 272 \times 2} \\
13\,600 + \quad {\scriptstyle 272 \times 50} \\
\hline
14\,144 \\
{\scriptstyle 1}
\end{array}
$$

Sarah earns £14 144 per year

Division

Dividing quite often produces a remainder and you will need to decide what is a sensible answer.

$$
\begin{array}{r}
7 \quad \text{remainder } 4 \\
6\overline{)46}
\end{array}
$$

Example

A baker is packing cakes in a box.
Each box can hold 6 cakes.
How many full boxes will the baker pack if he has 46 cakes?
How many cakes will be left over?

The baker will pack 7 full boxes and have 4 cakes left over.

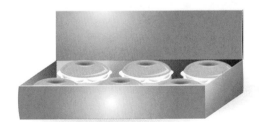

Multiplication and Division

Dividing a 3-Digit Number by a 2-Digit Number

Example

A bar of chocolate costs 63p. Jonathan has £9.57 to spend. What is the maximum number of chocolate bars that Jonathan can buy? How much change will he have left?

Method 1:

$$63\overline{)957}$$ with 15 above

Quotient: 15
```
    15
63)957
   63 -
   327
   315 -
    12
```

Step 1: 63 goes into 95 once, write down 1

Step 2: Subtract 63 from 95 (= 32)

Step 3: Bring down the 7 (= 327)

Step 4: 63 goes into 327 five times, write down 5

Step 5: 63 x 5 = 315

Step 6: 327 − 315 = 12. This is the remainder.

Method 2:

```
     15
63)957
   630 -
   327
   315 -
    12
```

Step 1: 630 (10 × 63) is less than 957, so 63 goes into 957 at least ten times

Step 2: Subtract 630 from 957 (= 327)

Step 3: 5 × 63 = 315, so 63 goes into 327 five times

Step 4: Subtract 315 from 327 (= 12)

Step 5: Add the 10 and 5 together, so 63 goes into 957 15 times, with a remainder of 12.

Jonathan can buy 15 chocolate bars and has 12p left over.

BIDMAS

BIDMAS helps you to remember the order for calculations.

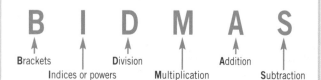

B — Brackets
I — Indices or powers
D — Division
M — Multiplication
A — Addition
S — Subtraction

The brackets are worked out first, then any powers, then division and multiplication are done before addition and subtraction.

Examples

Work out...

❶ $(5 + 3) \times 6$ ← Work out the brackets first.

$= 8 \times 6$

$= 48$

❷ $5 + 3 \times 6$ ← Carry out the multiplication first.

$= 5 + 18$

$= 23$

Multiples

Multiples are numbers that are in the multiplication tables.

Example
What are the multiples of 4?

Multiples of 4 are 4, 8, 12, 16, 20, ...

Factors

Factors are whole numbers that divide exactly into other whole numbers.

Example
What are the factors of 18?

The factors of 18 are: 1×18
2×9
3×6
i.e. 1, 2, 3, 6, 9, 18

Prime Numbers

A **prime number** has only two factors, 1 and itself.

The prime numbers up to 20 are 2, 3, 5, 7, 11, 13, 17 and 19.

Note that...
- 1 isn't a prime number
- 2 is the only even prime number.

Eratosthenes and Euclid

Eratosthenes was a Greek mathematician (276BC–194BC).

He's famous for devising a method for finding primes called the 'Sieve of Eratosthenes'.

Euclid, another Greek mathematician (c.330BC–260BC), proved that there are infinitely many prime numbers.

Square Numbers

Square numbers are whole numbers raised to the power 2.

For example...
$4^2 = 4 \times 4 = 16$ ('four squared')

The first 12 square numbers are:

1	**4**	**9**	**16**	**25**	**36**
(1 × 1)	(2 × 2)	(3 × 3)	(4 × 4)	(5 × 5)	(6 × 6)

49	**64**	**81**	**100**	**121**	**144**
(7 × 7)	(8 × 8)	(9 × 9)	(10 × 10)	(11 × 11)	(12 × 12)

Square numbers can be illustrated by drawing squares:

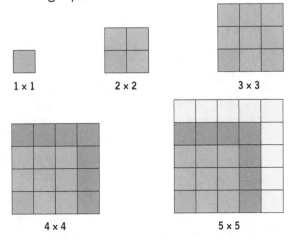

1 x 1   2 x 2   3 x 3

4 x 4   5 x 5

Cube Numbers

Cube numbers are whole numbers raised to the power 3.

For example...
$4^3 = 4 \times 4 \times 4 = 64$ ('four cubed')

This could be illustrated by drawing a cube:

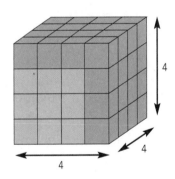

Some other cube numbers include:

1	**8**	**27**	**64**	**125**
(1 × 1 × 1)	(2 × 2 × 2)	(3 × 3 × 3)	(4 × 4 × 4)	(5 × 5 × 5)

Multiplication and Division

Triangular Numbers

The sequence of **triangular numbers** is 1, 3, 6, 10, 15, ...

With each step in the sequence, the difference goes up by 1.

Triangular numbers can be illustrated by drawing triangles.

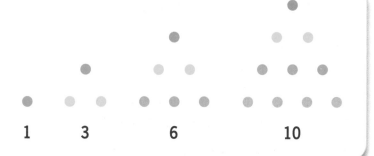

1   3   6   10

Square Roots

$\sqrt{}$ is the **square root** sign.

Taking the square root is the opposite of squaring.

For example, $\sqrt{36}$ = 6 or -6

since 6^2 = 36 and $(-6)^2$ = 36

Cube Roots

$\sqrt[3]{}$ is the **cube root** sign.

Taking the cube root is the opposite of cubing.

For example, $\sqrt[3]{27}$ = 3

since 3^3 = 3 × 3 × 3 = 27

Quick Test

1. Describe how you would multiply a number by 100.
2. Describe how you would divide a number by 1000.
3. What does the word 'product' mean?
4. Is the following multiplication true or false?
   675 × 23 = 15 525
5. The 'I' in BIDMAS stands for 'Indices' or 'Powers'? True or false?
6. How many factors does 24 have?
   A 10   **B** 6   **C** 8   **D** 4
7. What is a cube number?
8. The square root of 49 is 7 or -7. True or false?

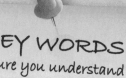

KEY WORDS
Make sure you understand these words before moving on!
- Product
- BIDMAS
- Multiple
- Factor
- Prime number
- Square number
- Cube number
- Triangular number
- Square root
- Cube root

1 Work out the answers to the following:
  a) 63×10 **c)** $270 \div 10$ **e)** 16×100
  b) 27×1000 **d)** $5900 \div 100$

2 A gymnast practises for 3 hours every day.
  For how many hours does she practise in a year?

3 A fruit grower has 110 apples to put into packets. Each packet holds 4 apples.
  a) How many packets can the fruit grower fill?
  b) How many apples are left over?

4 From the cloud of numbers, write down the…
  a) factors of 20   **c)** cube numbers   **e)** prime numbers.
  b) square numbers   **d)** multiples of 6

24 6 4
27 81
12
17   5   49   3
25   1   13   20

5 Work out…
  a) $7 + 2 \times 4$ **c)** $\sqrt[3]{125}$ **e)** 4^3
  b) $12 - (3 + 4)$ **d)** 6^2 **f)** $\sqrt{144}$

6 In a conference hall, there are 43 chairs per row.
  How many chairs in total are needed for 289 rows?

7 A train carriage can hold 126 people.
  If a train has 13 carriages, how many people can it hold?

8 Paperclips come in boxes of 54.
  An office needs 900 paperclips.
  How many boxes should be bought?

9 Cans of cola cost 64p each.
  Mark needs to buy as many cans as possible.
  He has £17.
  a) How many cans of cola can Mark buy?
  b) How much change will he get back?

The Sieve of Eratosthenes

- On a 100 square, cross out the number 1, since it isn't a prime number.
- Circle 2 and then cross out all other multiples of 2. The next number not crossed out is 3.
- Circle 3 and then cross out all other multiples of 3. The next number not crossed out is 5.
- Sircle 5 and then cross out all other multiples of 5. The next number not crossed out is 7.
- Continue the process until no more numbers can be circled.

The circled numbers are all the prime numbers less than 100.

Fractions

Fractions

A **fraction** is a whole unit divided into equal parts.

For example, $\frac{7}{9}$ means 7 parts out of 9:

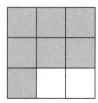

Fractions are used every day. An example is shown below:

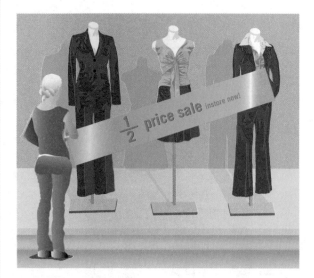

The top number is ⟶ the **numerator**.

The bottom number is ⟶ the **denominator**.

$$\frac{1}{2}$$

If the numerator is smaller than the denominator, it's called a **proper fraction**, for example, $\frac{7}{11}$

If the numerator is bigger than the denominator, it's called an **improper fraction**, for example, $\frac{12}{7}$

A fraction that has a whole number and a fraction is called a **mixed number**, for example, $3\frac{1}{2}$

Equivalent Fractions

Equivalent fractions are fractions that have the same value.

Fractions can be changed into their equivalent by either multiplying or dividing the numerator and denominator by the same number.

 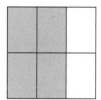

From the diagram, it can be seen that $\frac{2}{3} = \frac{4}{6}$

Examples
Complete the equivalent fractions:

1 $\frac{3}{11} = \frac{?}{44}$

$\times 4$

$$\frac{3}{11} = \frac{12}{44}$$

Multiply the numerator and denominator by 4.

$\times 4$

2 $\frac{50}{60} = \frac{5}{?}$

$\div 10$

$$\frac{50}{60} = \frac{5}{6}$$

Divide the numerator and denominator by 10.

$\div 10$

Simplifying Fractions

Fractions can be **simplified** if the numerator and denominator have a common factor. This process is called **cancelling**.

$\div 10$

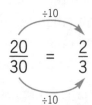

$$\frac{20}{30} = \frac{2}{3}$$

10 is the **highest common factor** of 20 and 30, so dividing the numerator and denominator by 10 gives $\frac{2}{3}$

$\div 10$

Adding and Subtracting Fractions

Only fractions with the same denominator can be added or subtracted.

Examples

① Work out $\frac{2}{3} + \frac{5}{6}$

The lowest common denominator (i.e. least common multiple of 3 and 6) is 6.

Therefore, change $\frac{2}{3}$ into an equivalent fraction with a denominator of 6.

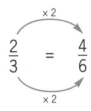

Now, rewrite the sum:

$$\frac{2}{3} + \frac{5}{6} = \frac{4}{6} + \frac{5}{6} = \frac{4+5}{6} = \frac{9}{6}$$

$$\frac{9}{6} = 1\frac{3}{6} = 1\frac{1}{2}$$ ⟵ Simplify the fraction.

$$\frac{2}{3} \quad + \quad \frac{5}{6} \quad = \quad 1 \quad \frac{1}{2}$$

② Work out $\frac{9}{10} - \frac{3}{5}$

$$\frac{9}{10} - \frac{3}{5} = \frac{9}{10} - \frac{6}{10} = \frac{3}{10}$$

10 is the lowest common denominator of 5 and 10.

Fractions of Quantities

To find a fraction of a quantity, you multiply the fraction with the quantity.

Examples

① Find $\frac{3}{8}$ of £24

Rewrite the question as $\frac{3}{8} \times 24$

$24 \div 8 = 3$ Divide 24 by 8; multiply by 3.
$3 \times 3 = 9$

So, $\frac{3}{8}$ of £24 is £9

② In a town of 12 000 households, $\frac{5}{6}$ recycle their rubbish.
Work out the number of households that recycle their rubbish.

$\frac{5}{6}$ of 12 000 is:

$\frac{5}{6} \times 12\,000 = 10\,000$ households

Quick Test

① The top number in a fraction is called the denominator. True or false?
② What is $\frac{21}{6}$ written as a mixed number?
  A $3\frac{1}{3}$ **B** $6\frac{2}{3}$ **C** $2\frac{1}{2}$ **D** $3\frac{1}{2}$
③ How would you work out $\frac{1}{4}$ of £16?
④ What is $\frac{3}{5} + \frac{4}{10}$?
  A $\frac{7}{15}$ **B** $\frac{7}{10}$ **C** 1 **D** $\frac{4}{10}$
⑤ The answer to $\frac{3}{5}$ of £20 is £12. True or false?

Fractions

Skills Practice

1 For each shape, write down...
  i) the fraction that's shaded
  ii) the fraction that's not shaded.

a) 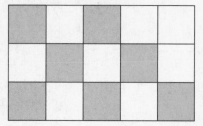   **b)** 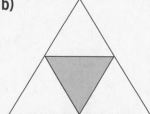   **c)**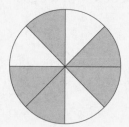

2 Copy this shape and shade in $\frac{5}{6}$.

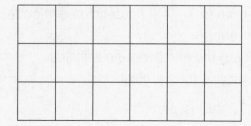

3 Copy and complete these fractions:
  a) $\frac{2}{3} = \frac{?}{12}$ **b)** $\frac{25}{30} = \frac{5}{?}$ **c)** $\frac{9}{12} = \frac{27}{?}$ **d)** $\frac{20}{36} = \frac{10}{?}$

4 The following cards show some fractions.

$$\frac{2}{3} \qquad \frac{4}{5} \qquad \frac{5}{9} \qquad \frac{12}{15} \qquad \frac{10}{15}$$

$$\frac{9}{10} \qquad \frac{21}{27} \qquad \frac{11}{32} \qquad \frac{25}{45} \qquad \frac{20}{40} \qquad \frac{7}{9}$$

Write down the fractions that are equivalent.

5 Work out...
  a) $\frac{2}{3} + \frac{1}{3}$ **c)** $\frac{2}{5} - \frac{3}{10}$ **e)** $\frac{12}{17} - \frac{3}{34}$
  b) $\frac{7}{9} - \frac{2}{9}$ **d)** $\frac{3}{8} + \frac{1}{16}$ **f)** $\frac{3}{10} + \frac{1}{2}$

6 Richard is designing his garden.
$\frac{2}{3}$ of the garden is grass and $\frac{1}{6}$ of the garden is a vegetable plot.
The rest of the garden is a flower bed.
What fraction of the garden is the flower bed?

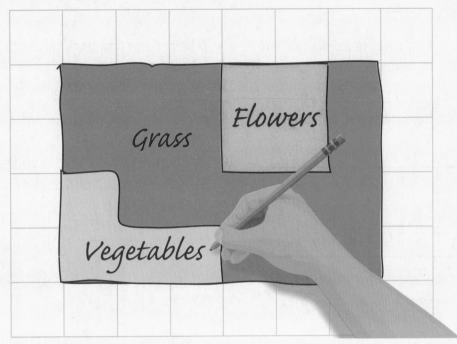

7 An architect is designing a play area.
$\frac{1}{5}$ of the area will be a children's playground.
$\frac{3}{10}$ of the area will be a swimming pool.
How much of the area has the architect used and how much is left?

8 Find...
   a) $\frac{2}{3}$ of 30ml   **b)** $\frac{5}{7}$ of 49kg   **c)** $\frac{3}{8}$ of £40

9 Find...
   a) $\frac{7}{12}$ of 1200kg   **b)** $\frac{8}{9}$ of £81   **c)** $\frac{7}{10}$ of £640

10 Rupinder gets £10 pocket money per week.
She spends $\frac{3}{5}$ of her pocket money on magazines.
How much does Rupinder spend on magazines each week?

11 John's mobile phone package includes 500 minutes
and 350 text messages per month.
In February, he used $\frac{4}{5}$ of his inclusive minutes
and $\frac{3}{7}$ of his text message allowance.
   a) How many of his inclusive minutes did John
      not use in February?
   b) How many text messages did John send?

12 Jessica wrote down the following sum:

$\frac{2}{3} + \frac{4}{5} = \frac{6}{8}$

Show whether or not Jessica is correct.

Decimals

Decimals

Decimals are used for parts of numbers that are less than 1.

A **decimal point** is used to separate whole number columns from fractional columns. For example...

Thousands	Hundreds	Tens	Units	Decimal Point	Tenths	Hundredths	Thousandths
9	5	4	3	•	8	7	2

Max Depth 1.1m

- The column headings tell us the place value of each figure.
- The 7 has a value of $\frac{7}{100}$ (seven hundredths).

Decimals are used every day, for example...
- digital thermometers
- height restrictions (e.g. a bridge with a height restriction of 4.2m)
- swimming pools.

Recurring Decimals

A decimal that **recurs** is shown by placing a dot over the number that repeats.

If more than one number is repeated, place a dot over the first and last number in the recurring sequence.

Example
Write 0.474747... as a recurring decimal.

$0.474747... = 0.\dot{4}\dot{7}$

Converting between Decimals and Fractions

When converting decimals into fractions, use the place values of the figures.

Example
Write 0.35 as a fraction.

$0.35 = \frac{3}{10} + \frac{5}{100} = \frac{30}{100} + \frac{5}{100} = \frac{35}{100}$

When converting fractions into decimals, divide the numerator by the denominator.

Example
Convert $\frac{3}{5}$ into a decimal.

$\frac{3}{5} = 3 \div 5 = 0.6$

Multiplying Decimals by 10, 100 and 1000

- To multiply a decimal number by 10, move each digit one place to the left.
- To multiply a decimal number by 100, move each digit two places to the left.
- To multiply a decimal number by 1000, move each digit three places to the left.

Examples
1. $16.93 \times 10 = 169.3$
2. $273.61 \times 100 = 27\,361$
3. $0.294 \times 1000 = 294$

Dividing Decimals by 10, 100 and 1000

- To divide a decimal number by 10, move each digit one place to the right.
- To divide a decimal number by 100, move each digit two places to the right.
- To divide a decimal number by 1000, move each digit three places to the right.

Examples
1. $25.62 \div 10 = 2.562$
2. $71.3 \div 100 = 0.713$
3. $493.7 \div 1000 = 0.4937$

Adding, Subtracting, Multiplying and Dividing Decimals

The methods used to add, subtract, multiply and divide whole numbers can also be used for decimals.

Examples
Work out...

1. $27.93 + 14.62$

```
  27.93
  14.62 +
  42.55
  1 1
```

It's important that you line up the digits carefully.

So, $27.93 + 14.62 = 42.55$

2. $89.6 - 41.37$

```
  89.60
  41.37 −
  48.23
```

Fill in the zero after the 6 tenths.

So, $89.6 - 41.37 = 48.23$

3. 7.39×5

```
  7.39
     5 ×
  36.95
   1 4
```

Multiply each of the digits 7, 3 and 9 by 5, starting from the right and moving to the left.

So, $7.39 \times 5 = 36.95$

4. 2.63×45

This requires long multiplication. It's made easier if you first multiply 2.63 by 100 to remove the decimal point:

```
    263
     45 ×
   1315      ← 263 x 5
  10520 +    ← 263 x 40
  11835
```

The answer now needs to be divided by 100, because you multiplied by 100 originally:

$11\,835 \div 100 = 118.35$

5. $25.5 \div 5$

```
      5.1
  5)25.5
```

Make sure that the decimal points are lined up.

So, $25.5 \div 5 = 5.1$

6. $47.4 \div 0.2$

$47.4 \div 0.2$ is equivalent to $474 \div 2$ (multiplying both numbers by 10):

```
     237
  2)474
```

So, $47.4 \div 0.2 = 237$

Decimals

Rounding Decimals

It's sometimes useful to round decimals to the nearest whole number, or to a given number of decimal places.

To round to the nearest whole number, look at the number in the first decimal place:
- If it is 5 or more, round the units up to the next whole number.
- If it is less than 5, the units stay the same.

Examples
1. 6.3 = 6 (to the nearest whole number)
2. 12.5mm = 13mm (to the nearest whole number)

To round to the nearest tenth (one decimal place), look at the number in the second decimal place and follow the same rules as above.

Examples
1. 12.35 is 12.4 (to 1 d.p.)
2. 14.23 is 14.2 (to 1 d.p.)

A similar method can be used when rounding any number to a particular number of decimal places.

Examples
1. 15.675 = 15.68 (to 2 d.p.)
2. 9.363 = 9.36 (to 2 d.p.)

Measurements are rounded to different degrees of accuracy depending on the circumstance.

In a school sports event, the time taken to run the 100m is likely to be rounded to one decimal place, whereas at International Level it's rounded to two decimal places.

Rounding can have a big impact. This article shows how important rounding is:

100 METRE WORLD RECORD BLUNDER

American sprinter Justin Gatlin's hopes of being named the world's fastest man have been dashed following news that his record-breaking time of 9.76 seconds will not count.

GUTTED
Gatlin was told that he'd beaten Asafa Powell's 9.77 second record by one one-hundredth of a second in Qatar. However, the sport's officials have now announced that he actually clocked 9.766 seconds, not 9.760 as first announced.

According to the rules of the IAAF, the world governing body for track and field, Gatlin's time should've been rounded up to 9.77 seconds, only equalling – not beating – the record already set by Powell.

Quick Test

1. In the number 639.465 what is the place value of the digit 5?
2. The decimal 0.27 written as a fraction is $\frac{27}{100}$. True or false?
3. What is 83.62 – 14.79?
   A 67.83   **B** 68.83   **C** 71.17   **D** 69.37
4. What is 25.6 × 31?
5. When rounding a number to the nearest tenth, which number do you look at?

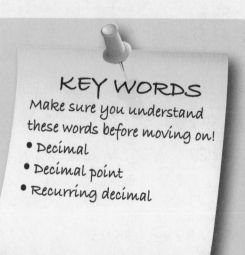

KEY WORDS
Make sure you understand these words before moving on!
- Decimal
- Decimal point
- Recurring decimal

Skills Practice

1. Write down the value of the underlined digit in each decimal number.
   a) 62.<u>3</u>
   b) 4.0<u>7</u>
   c) 15<u>6</u>.231
   d) 27.26<u>4</u>

2. Work out...
   a) 27.6 × 10
   b) 493.2 ÷ 100
   c) 96.3 × 100
   d) 294.3 ÷ 1000
   e) 16.2 × 1000
   f) 2.9 ÷ 10

3. Work out...
   a) 27.6 + 491.3
   b) 273.69 – 12.7
   c) 28.6 × 4
   d) 211.5 ÷ 5
   e) 14.3 × 12
   f) 13.5 ÷ 0.3

4. Work out...
   a) 271.6 + 45.3
   b) 279.4 – 102.6
   c) 37.4 × 9
   d) 515.65 ÷ 5
   e) 18.6 × 17
   f) 48.8 ÷ 0.4

5. Rebecca took part in a triathlon.
   She ran 1.8km, swam 0.24km and cycled 2.241km.
   How far in total did Rebecca travel?

6. Mohammed sawed 0.38 metres off a one-metre long piece of wood.
   Work out the length of wood left over.

7. Find the total cost, in pounds (£), of four loaves of bread costing £0.92 each and seven cans of cola at £0.55 each.

8. Find the total cost, in pounds (£), of 26 train tickets costing £9.62 each.

9. A piece of rope is 4.72m long.
   If Mr Percy cuts off 2.31m from the rope, how much will be left?

10. Round these numbers to one decimal place:
    a) 6.49
    b) 7.43
    c) 5.65
    d) 4.27

11. Round these numbers to two decimal places:
    a) 3.527
    b) 16.653
    c) 127.425
    d) 4.692
    e) 12.685
    f) 37.255
    g) 38.471
    h) 38.528
    i) 37.725

12. Charlotte jumped 1.4 metres (correct to one decimal place) in a long jump competition.
    What's the minimum possible distance that Charlotte could have jumped?

Negative Numbers

Negative Numbers

Positive numbers are above zero and **negative numbers** are below zero.

Negative numbers are written with the minus sign in front of the digits, for example, -13.

Temperatures often use positive and negative numbers.

The weather map opposite shows the temperature on one day in December. Edinburgh has a temperature of -3°C and London has a temperature of 2°C.

It's predicted that the average temperature is set to rise by between 1 and 4 degrees by the end of the century, due to global warming.

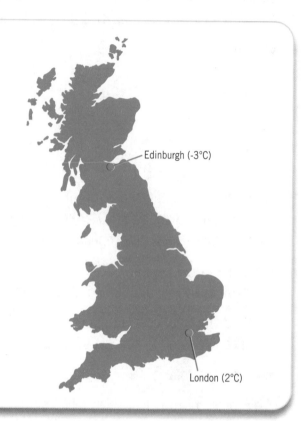

Edinburgh (-3°C)

London (2°C)

Ordering Positive and Negative Numbers

This is a number line:

Negative | Positive

-10 -9 -8 -7 -6 -5 -4 -3 -2 -1 0 1 2 3 4 5 6 7 8 9 10

As the numbers go to the **left**, they get **smaller** (e.g. -9 is smaller than -2).

As the numbers go to the **right**, they get **bigger** (e.g. 7 is bigger than -4).

Examples

1. Place these numbers in order of size, smallest first: 6, -3, -7, 2, 0, 12, -5, -1

The order is -7, -5, -3, -1, 0, 2, 6, 12.

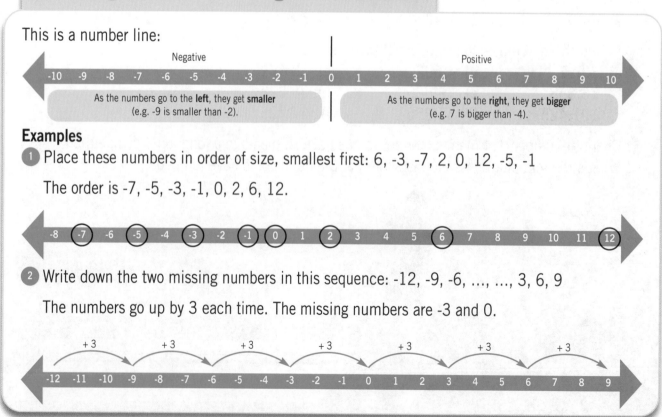

2. Write down the two missing numbers in this sequence: -12, -9, -6, ..., ..., 3, 6, 9

The numbers go up by 3 each time. The missing numbers are -3 and 0.

Adding and Subtracting Positive and Negative Numbers

Example

The temperature at 4am was -3°C. By 11am it had risen by 9°C.
What is the new temperature?

-3 + 9 = 6°C   A number line can be used to help when adding and subtracting positive and negative numbers.

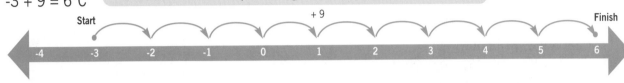

Adding and Subtracting Negative Numbers

When two negative numbers are added together, the result is a negative number.

For example, -6 + -2 is the same as -6 – 2 = -8

When you subtract numbers, you find the difference between them.

For example, 3 – -5 = 8

The difference between 3 and -5 is 8.

Hence, subtracting a negative number has the same effect as adding a positive number.
For example, -3 – -4 becomes -3 + 4 = 1

Quick Test

1. -6 is smaller than -5. True or false?
2. -8 is smaller than -10. True or false?
3. The temperature at 9am is 3°C. By 9pm it has
   fallen by 7°C. What is the temperature at 9pm?
   A -3°C **B** -4°C **C** -5°C **D** 4°C
4. When subtracting a negative number, it has
   the same effect as adding a negative number.
   True or false?
5. What is 6 – -3?
   A 3   **B** -3   **C** 9   **D** -9
6. What is the missing number in the sequence
   -7, -5, ..., -1, 1, 3, 5, 7?
   A -4   **B** -3   **C** -2   **D** 0

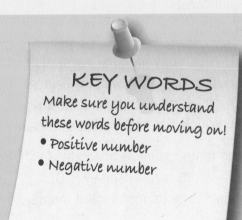

KEY WORDS
Make sure you understand
these words before moving on!
• Positive number
• Negative number

Negative Numbers

1. For each list, write down...
    i) the highest temperature
    ii) the lowest temperature.
   a) 6°C, -5°C, 4°C, 7°C, -3°C, 0°C
   b) -5°C, -4°C, 2°C, -6°C, 1°C, -3°C
   c) -9°C, 4°C, 7°C, 0°C, -6°C, -2°C
   d) -12°C, 6°C, 7°C, -3°C, 14°C, -1°C
   e) 13°C, -4°C, -7°C, 6°C, 5°C, -8°C
   f) -9°C, 9°C, 0°C, 6°C, -7°C, 10°C

2. Write each set of temperatures in order of size, starting with the lowest.
   a) 5°C, -3°C, 6°C, -2°C, 0°C, 4°C
   b) -7°C, -2°C, 3°C, -9°C, 5°C
   c) 2°C, -5°C, 12°C, -10°C, 9°C, 4°C
   d) 7°C, -4°C, 9°C, 0°C, -6°C, -1°C
   e) -12°C, 7°C, 14°C, 9°C, -5°C, -2°C
   f) -8°C, 6°C, 12°C, -1°C, 9°C, -3°C

3. The table shows the temperature at midnight and midday on one day in five cities.

City	Midnight Temperature (°C)	Midday Temperature (°C)
Dublin	-3	6
Glasgow	-5	7
London	2	8
Manchester	-2	7
Cardiff	1	12

   a) Which city had the lowest midnight temperature?
   b) At midnight, how many degrees higher was the temperature in London than in Glasgow?
   c) Which city had the smallest rise in temperature from midnight to midday?
   d) Which city had the largest rise in temperature from midnight to midday?

4. The temperature at midnight is -6°C.
   By midday it has risen by 8°C.
   What is the temperature at midday?

5. Find the value of each of the following:
   a) 6 – 9
   b) -7 + 2
   c) -3 + 4
   d) -7 – 2
   e) 5 – 12
   f) 16 – 26
   g) 3 – 4
   h) -4 + 8
   i) -127 + 200
   j) -7 + 2
   k) -6 – 10
   l) 8 – 15

6 Write down the next two numbers in each of these patterns:

a) 7, 4, 1, -2, ..., ...

b) -7, -5, -3, -1, ..., ...

c) -2, -4, -6, -8, ..., ...

7 Work out...

a) 2 – -5

b) 3 – -4

c) -2 – -3

d) 5 + -2

e) -7 – -6

f) -12 + -4

g) 6 + -10

h) -10 – -5

i) 2 – -7

j) 7 – -2

k) -5 + -2

l) 9 + -3

m) 5 – -1

n) -3 + -2

o) -7 – -5

8 A number pyramid is completed by adding two cells to give the number in the cells above. For example:

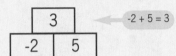

-2 + 5 = 3

Copy and complete the number pyramids below.

a)
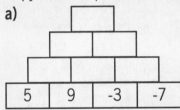

c)
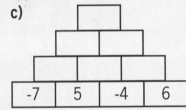

e)
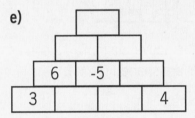

b)
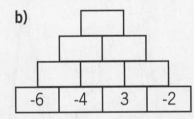

d)
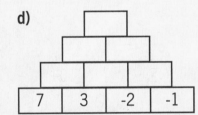

f)
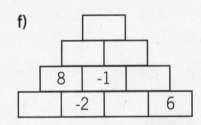

9 Copy and complete these arithmagons.

On each side of the arithmagon, the total of the numbers in the circles goes in the squares between them.

a)
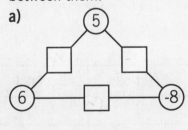

c)
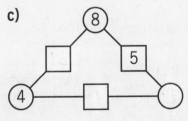

e)
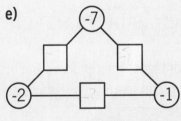

b)
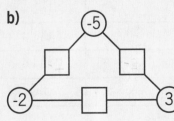

d)
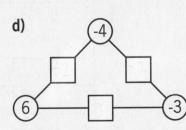

f)
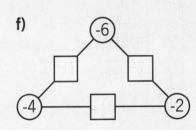

Percentages

Percentages

A **percentage** is equivalent to a **fraction** with a **denominator** of 100.

Percentage means 'out of 100'. The symbol % is the percentage sign.

For example, 12% means $\frac{12}{100}$:

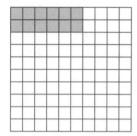

In the above diagram, 12 squares out of 100 are shaded (12%).

Example

A flag has two colours: red and green. If 30% of the flag is red, what percentage is green?

Percentage green = 100% – 30%
= 70%

Percentages are often seen in everyday life, as in the examples opposite.

Percentages, Fractions and Decimals

Percentages, fractions and **decimals** are related. You should learn these simple **equivalents**.

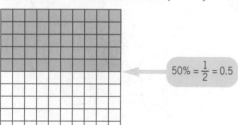

$50\% = \frac{1}{2} = 0.5$

Percentages	Fractions	Decimals
75%	$\frac{3}{4}$	0.75
50%	$\frac{1}{2}$	0.5
25%	$\frac{1}{4}$	0.25
10%	$\frac{1}{10}$	0.1
1%	$\frac{1}{100}$	0.01

Percentages of a Quantity (1)

Using a non-calculator method

When finding a percentage of a quantity without using a calculator, 10% is the easiest percentage to work out. This is because 10% is the same as one tenth.

Finding one tenth is the same as dividing by 10.

Examples
Find...

1 10% of £220

10% is £220 ÷ 10
= £22

2 20% of £44

10% is £44 ÷ 10
= £4.40

20% is £4.40 × 2
= £8.80

> Once you know 10%, you can find 20% by multiplying by 2.

3 5% of £60

10% is £60 ÷ 10
= £6

5% is £6 ÷ 2
= £3

> 5% is one half of 10%

Example
VAT (Value Added Tax) is a tax you pay on the cost of items bought.
VAT is charged at 20%.
Find the VAT on a coat that costs £80.

20% = 10% + 10% (or 10% × 2)

10% of £80 is £80 ÷ 10
= £8

So, VAT charged on a coat costing £80 is
£8 + £8 = £16

The actual price of the coat including VAT is
£80 + £16 = £96

Percentages of a Quantity (2)

Using a calculator

When finding a percentage of a quantity using a calculator, multiply the quantity by the percentage and divide by 100.

Example
Find 23% of £60

Key in:

$\frac{23}{100} \times £60 = £13.80$

Percentages of a Quantity (3)

Problems

Problems can be solved using percentages of a quantity.

Example
A school raises £12 000 in a gala event.
30% of the money is given to charity.
How much is given to charity?

You need to find 30% of £12 000:

$\frac{30}{100} \times £12\,000 = £3600$

£3600 is given to charity.

Percentages

Percentage Increase and Decrease

Increases and decreases are often given in percentages.

Examples

1 In a sale, all prices are reduced by 15%. Find the sale price of a jacket that originally cost £80.

10%   is £80 ÷ 10
       = £8

  5%   is £8 ÷ 2
       = £4

15%   is £8 + £4
       = £12

Jacket costs £80 − £12 = £68

2 Tracey earns £45 000 per year. She gets a 2% pay rise. How much does Tracey earn after her pay rise?

First, you need to find 2% of £45 000:

$\frac{2}{100} \times £45\,000 = £900$

So, salary after pay rise is £45 000 + £900
                                     = £45 900

Quick Test

1 What is the percentage sign?
2 Explain how you would find 10% of a quantity.
3 What is 30% of £60?
   A £9   **B** £18   **C** £24   **D** £6
4 Explain how you would work out 37% of £70 using a calculator.
5 Katie earns £35 000 per year.
   She pays 22% tax on her earnings.
   How much tax does Katie pay in a year?
   A £7700   **C** £7000
   B £27 300   **D** £28 000
6 A television costs £500.
   In a sale it's reduced by 15%.
   How much does the television cost now?
   A £50   **B** £75   **C** £450 **D** £425

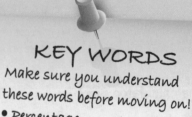

KEY WORDS
Make sure you understand these words before moving on!
• Percentage
• Fraction
• Denominator
• Decimal
• Equivalent

1 What percentage of each shape is shaded?

a)

b)

c)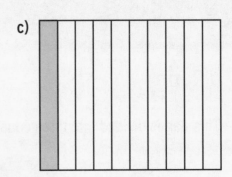

2 A class of students is made up of 54% girls.
What percentage of the class is male?

3 In a class of students, 27% are left-handed whilst the rest are right-handed.
What percentage of the students are right-handed?

4 From the money raised by a fun run, 65% is given to a local hospice and the rest is used to buy a school minibus.
What percentage of the money is used to buy the minibus?

5 Find...
   a) 10% of 70kg
   b) 20% of £140
   c) 30% of 50mm
   d) 60% of £240
   e) 40% of £80
   f) 30% of £90
   g) 65% of £120
   h) 35% of £150

6 Using a calculator, find...
   a) 12% of 850km
   b) 72% of £800
   c) 13% of 48kg
   d) 6% of £12.50
   e) 15% of £650
   f) 28% of 270m
   g) 36% of £82
   h) 64% of 350kg

7 The 60 girls in Year 8 were asked to choose their favourite sport.
70% of the girls chose netball.
Work out how many girls chose netball.

8 35% of students walk to school.
If there are 1200 students at a school,
how many walk to get there?

9 Robert had £560 in his savings account.
He left the money in the account for one year.
Interest was paid at 6% per year.
   a) Calculate the interest paid to Robert at the end of the year.
   b) At the end of the year, how much did Robert have altogether?

10 Perlita bought a CD in a sale.
The original price of the CD was £12.
In the sale, the price of the CD was reduced by 20%.
How much did Perlita pay for the CD?

Ratio

Ratio

This flag is divided into three equal parts:

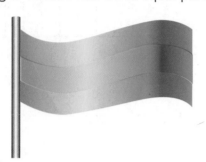

Two of the parts are coloured red and one part is coloured green:
- The **ratio** of red to green is 2 : 1
- The ratio of green to red is 1 : 2

The colon means 'compared to'.

A ratio is a way of comparing two or more related quantities.

Example

In a maths class, 17 students are girls and 13 students are boys.

a) What is the ratio of boys to girls?

   The ratio of boys to girls is 13 : 17

b) What is the ratio of girls to boys?

   The ratio of girls to boys is 17 : 13

c) What fraction of the class is girls?

   There are 30 students altogether.

   $\frac{17}{30}$ of the students are girls.

Equivalent Ratios

Ratios are **equivalent** when they represent the same relationship. The units must be the same.

Example

Dermot is making some fruit punch for a party. He mixes 200ml of orange juice with 800ml of cranberry juice.

Write this as a ratio in its simplest form.

The ratio is:

Orange : Cranberry

$\div 200$ 200 : 800 $\div 200$

1 : 4

Simplifying Ratios

A ratio in its **simplest form** is also said to be in its **lowest terms**.

For example, the ratio 200 : 800 is equivalent to the ratio 1 : 4.

Calculating with Ratios

A common way to solve ratio problems is to reduce one of the ratios to one, and then find what one quantity is worth.

Examples

1 It costs £1.50 for 3 metres of tape. How much would 7 metres of tape cost?

3 metres cost £1.50

1 metre costs £1.50 ÷ 3
= £0.50

7 metres cost 7 × £0.50
= £3.50

2 A box of 8 pens costs £2.24
How much will 12 pens cost?

8 pens cost £2.24

1 pen costs £2.24 ÷ 8
= £0.28 In other words, one pen costs 28p

12 pens cost 12 × 28p
= £3.36

3 A bottle of blackcurrant squash carries the following mixing instructions:

Just mix 1 part of juice with 6 parts of water for a refreshing drink

a) How much water should Ray add to five centilitres of juice?

There needs to be six times as much water as juice:
6 × 5 = 30
There needs to be 30 centilitres of water

b) What quantity of juice should Ray add to one litre of water?

1 litre = 100 centilitres of water

There should be one-sixth as much juice as water:
100 ÷ 6 = 16.7
There should be 16.7 centilitres of juice

Quick Test

1 What is a ratio?
2 The ratio 20 : 15 fully simplified is 4 : 3. True or false?
3 What is the ratio 48 : 24 when fully simplified?
    A 12 : 6 **B** 6 : 12 **C** 1 : 2 **D** 2 : 1
4 7 pencils cost 98p. What is the cost of 18 pencils?
    A 14p **B** £2.52 **C** £1.40 **D** £2.60
5 When are ratios equivalent?

KEY WORDS
Make sure you understand these words before moving on!
- Ratio
- Equivalent
- Simplest form
- Lowest terms

Ratio

1. For each of these shapes, what is the ratio of red parts to green parts?

    a)

    b)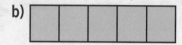

    c)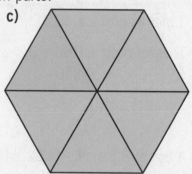

2. Write each of these ratios in their simplest form:

    a) 3 : 6
    b) 5 : 10
    c) 200 : 500
    d) 200 : 100

    e) 75 : 35
    f) 50 : 55
    g) 24 : 18
    h) 16 : 22

    i) 25 : 55
    j) 75 : 30
    k) 64 : 4
    l) 27 : 81

3. Write these ratios in their lowest terms:

    a) 20cm : 10mm
    b) 40cm : 2m
    c) 1 hour : 30 minutes

    d) £5 : 200p
    e) 5km : 100cm
    f) 3 hours : 45 minutes

    g) £6 : 30p
    h) 50cm : 2m
    i) 5000g : 1kg

4. Pewter contains lead and tin in the ratio 20 : 80.
   Write this ratio in its simplest form.

5. A mega-chip cookie contains milk, plain and white chocolate chips in the ratio 5 : 10 : 25.
   Write this ratio in its simplest form.

6. In one month, there were 14 sunny days and 16 wet days.
   Find the ratio of wet days to sunny days.

7. In a bag of counters, there are 7 blue counters and 28 red counters.
   Find the ratio of blue to red counters.

8. In a survey of cars, 250 cars were silver, 80 were red and 50 were blue.
   Find the ratio of silver to red to blue cars.

9 In a wood, there are 65 beech trees, 45 conifers and 75 oak trees.
Find the ratio of beech trees to conifers to oak trees.

10 Sara buys six packets of seeds for £12.
How much would Sara pay for nine packets of seeds?

11 Three packs of A4 paper cost £6.51
How much does 13 packs of A4 paper cost?

12 12 sheets of paper are photocopied at a cost of £1.08
How much would it cost to photocopy 75 sheets of paper?

13 Molly is decorating three rooms.
The areas of the rooms are $30m^2$, $15m^2$ and $45m^2$.
Molly knows that a tin of paint covers $32m^2$.
How many tins of paint does Molly need to buy if she is painting each room with two coats?

14 70 maths books cost £805.
Work out the cost of buying...
a) 45 maths books   **b)** 123 maths books.

15 At a bank, Bobby changes £60 into 114 American dollars.
a) How many American dollars would Bobby get for changing £85 at this rate?
b) How many American dollars would Bobby get for changing £205 at this rate?

16 Rashna earns £142.80 for working 17 hours.
How much will Rashna earn if she works...
a) 15 hours?   **b)** 27 hours?   **c)** 36 hours?

17 A car drives steadily for 8 hours covering 304 miles.
a) How far has the car travelled after 6 hours?
b) How far has the car travelled after 11 hours?

Number Patterns

Number Patterns

A **number pattern** is a list or series of numbers that are connected by a rule.

You need to be able to recognise a number pattern and see how it builds up.

Another name for a number pattern is a **sequence**. Each value in the list of numbers is called a **term**.

When finding a missing term in a number pattern, look to see what's happening in the gap between previous terms.

Examples

1 2, 4, 6, 8, 10, ...
+2 +2 +2 +2

> The rule for this pattern is to add 2 each time.

2 5, 15, 45, 135, ...
×3 ×3 ×3

> The rule for this pattern is to multiply the previous term by 3.

3 20, 17, 14, 11, 8, 5, ...
−3 −3 −3 −3 −3

> The rule for this pattern is to subtract 3 each time.

Special Number Patterns

There are some special number patterns that you need to be able to recognise:

- 1, 4, 9, 16, 25, ...
  these are square numbers
- 1, 8, 27, 64, 125, ...
  these are cube numbers
- 2, 4, 8, 16, 32, ...
  these are the powers of 2
- 1, 3, 6, 10, 15, ...
  these are the triangular numbers

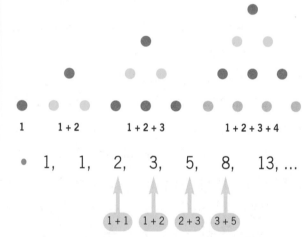

1   1 + 2   1 + 2 + 3   1 + 2 + 3 + 4

- 1, 1, 2, 3, 5, 8, 13, ...

1 + 1   1 + 2   2 + 3   3 + 5

this is known as the Fibonacci sequence. The rule is to add the two previous numbers each time.

Who was Fibonacci?

Fibonacci's real name was Leonardo of Pisa. He lived about 1175AD–1250AD.

Fibonacci is often called 'the greatest European mathematician of the Middle Ages' because of his contributions to mathematics.

He was one of the first people to introduce the Hindu-Arabic number system into Europe – the positional system, based on ten digits and the decimal point, used today.

Fibonacci introduced the Fibonacci sequence when looking at the breeding of rabbits.

Many aspects of nature are linked by the Fibonacci sequence.

Number Patterns in Diagrams

Number patterns can be seen in diagrams.

Example

The patterns below are made up of sticks.

4 sticks

7 sticks

10 sticks

13 sticks

Draw the next pattern in the sequence.

First, work out the rule to go from one pattern to the next. The rule is to add on 3 sticks each time.

So, the next pattern looks like this:

16 sticks

Number Machines

Number machines can be used to make number patterns.

When a number pattern is put into a number machine, the output numbers also make a pattern.

Input		Output

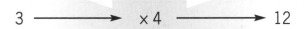

3 ⟶ × 4 ⟶ 12

Quick Test

1. Explain what the rule to this number pattern is:

   7, 10, 13, 16, ...

2. Explain what the Fibonacci sequence is.

3. What is the fourth square number?

   A 4

   B 9

   C 25

   D 16

4. 216 is a cube number. True or false?

5. What is the next number in this sequence?

   128, 64, 32, 16, ...

   A 8

   B 4

   C 12

   D 10

6. What is the output from this number machine?

7 ⟶ × 2   − 1 ⟶ ?

A 12

B 15

C 16

D 13

KEY WORDS

Make sure you understand these words before moving on!

- Number pattern
- Sequence
- Term

Number Patterns

1 For each sequence, write down...

   i) the next two numbers

   ii) the rule for finding the next number.

  a) 2, 4, 6, 8, ...   **e)** 30, 25, 20, 15, ...

  b) 5, 9, 13, 17, ...   **f)** 9, 18, 27, 36, ...

  c) 10, 7, 4, 1, ...   **g)** 70, 60, 50, 40, ...

  d) 64, 32, 16, 8, ...   **h)** 20, 40, 80, 160, ...

2 For each sequence, fill in the two missing terms and write down the rule that the sequence follows.

  a) 3, 6, 9, ..., ..., 18   **e)** 60, 54, 48, 42, ..., ..., 24

  b) 9, 13, 17, ..., ..., 29   **f)** 1, 4, 9, ..., ..., 36

  c) 48, 45, 42, ..., ..., 33   **g)** 1, 2, 4, 7, ..., ..., 22

  d) ..., ..., 26, 21, 16, 11   **h)** 3, 6, 12, ..., ..., 96

3 Here is a sequence of shapes made up of squares.

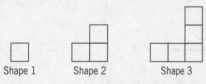

Shape 1   Shape 2   Shape 3

  a) Draw the next two shapes in the sequence.

  b) Copy and complete the following table:

Shape	1	2	3	4	5
Number of squares	1	3			

  c) How many squares will there be in shape 9?

  d) How many squares will there be in shape 25?

4 Look at this sequence of shapes made up of matchsticks:

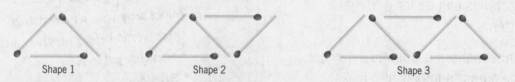

Shape 1   Shape 2   Shape 3

  a) Draw the next shape in the sequence.

  b) Copy and complete the following table:

Shape	1	2	3	4
Matchsticks				

  c) Write down the rule to go from one shape to the next.

5 This sequence is the first seven terms of the Fibonacci sequence:

1, 1, 2, 3, 5, 8, 13, ...

Continue the sequence up to, and including, the 15th term.

6 For each of the function tables below, write down what happens to the input in order to get the output.

a)

Input	Output
3	8
7	12
9	14

c)

Input	Output
2	4
7	14
4	8

e)

Input	Output
16	4
64	16
8	2

b)

Input	Output
7	5
12	10
4	2

d)

Input	Output
12	4
24	8
6	2

f)

Input	Output
2	5
5	11
9	19

7 For each of the number machines below...

   i) input the number pattern 2, 4, 6, 8

   ii) list the output numbers

   iii) describe the pattern it produces.

a)

$\times 5$

c)

$\times 2$ $+ 3$

b)

$+ 6$

d)

$\times 3$ $- 2$

8 Begin a sequence by writing the number 8.

Add 4 to give the 2nd term.

Add 4 to the 2nd term to give the 3rd term.

Continue until you have found the first 6 terms in the sequence.

9 Write down the first five terms of four different number patterns that each begin 1, 2, ...

Extension

Find an example of where the Fibonacci sequence occurs in nature.

Working with Algebra

Algebra

Algebra is an area of mathematics in which letters are used to represent values.

Algebra is used to solve many mathematical problems.

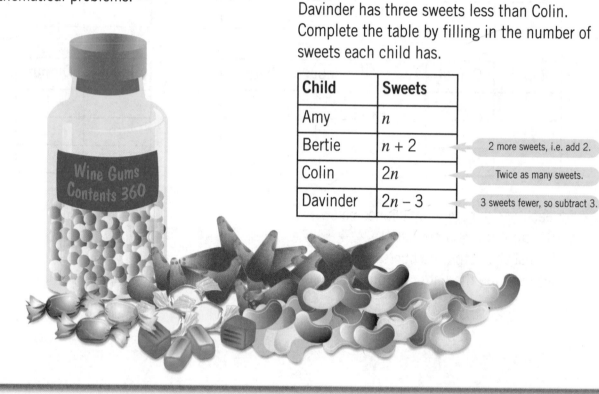

Example

Amy has n sweets.
Bertie has two more sweets than Amy.
Colin has twice as many sweets as Amy.
Davinder has three sweets less than Colin.
Complete the table by filling in the number of sweets each child has.

Child	Sweets
Amy	n
Bertie	$n + 2$
Colin	$2n$
Davinder	$2n - 3$

2 more sweets, i.e. add 2.

Twice as many sweets.

3 sweets fewer, so subtract 3.

Terms and Expressions

A **term** is a number, a letter, or a combination of numbers and letters multiplied together:

- Terms are separated by + or – signs.
- Each + or – sign is joined to the term that follows it.

$$+\ 6ab\ -\ 3b\ +\ 5$$

ab term with an invisible plus sign in front of it

b term

Number term

A **coefficient** is a number multiplying an algebraic term. In the example above, the coefficient of ab is 6 and the coefficient of b is 3.

A collection of terms is known as an **expression**.

You should follow these rules when writing expressions:

- A single a is written as a, not $1a$
- $a \times b$ is written as ab
- $a \times 2 \times b$ is written as $2ab$, that is, with the number first and the letters in alphabetical order
- $n \div 3$ is written as $\dfrac{n}{3}$

Collecting Like Terms

Expressions can be simplified by collecting like terms.

Like terms have the same letters and powers.

Examples

1. $5x + 4x = 9x$
2. $3y - y + 7y = 9y$
3. $5xy + 3yx = 8xy$ ← *xy and yx mean the same thing.*
4. $5a + 4b - a + 6b = 4a + 10b$

The minus is part of the a.

Add the a terms, then the b terms.

Multiplying Terms Together

Algebraic expressions are often simplified by multiplying terms together.

Examples

1. $3x \times 4y$
   $= 3 \times 4 \times x \times y$
   $= 12xy$

2. $5a \times 2b \times 3c$
   $= 5 \times 2 \times 3 \times a \times b \times c$
   $= 30abc$

Powers in Algebra

x^4 means $x \times x \times x \times x$

This is said as 'x to the power four'.

Similarly, $y^6 = y \times y \times y \times y \times y \times y$

Examples
Simplify these expressions using powers:

1. $2x \times 3y \times x$
   $= 2 \times x \times 3 \times y \times x$
   $= 6x^2y$

2. $b \times 2b \times 3b$
   $= 6b^3$

Multiplying out Single Brackets

Brackets are often used in algebra.

For example, $5 \times (x + y)$ is usually written as $5(x + y)$.

Multiplying out brackets is known as 'expanding the brackets'.

To expand brackets, each term inside the brackets is multiplied by the term outside the brackets.

Examples
Expand...

1. $5(a + b)$
   $= 5 \times a + 5 \times b$
   $= 5a + 5b$

2. $3(a - 4)$
   $= 3 \times a - 3 \times 4$
   $= 3a - 12$

3. $x(2x + 3y)$
   $= x \times 2x + x \times 3y$
   $= 2x^2 + 3xy$

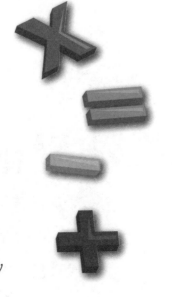

Working with Algebra

Using Word Formulae

A **formula** connects two expressions that contain **variables**.

The value of one variable depends on the values of the others.

A formula must contain an equals sign.

Science uses a lot of formulae. For example, a formula you may use in Physics is…

Force	=	Mass	×	Acceleration

Example
Sukhvinder buys some sweets. She uses this formula:

Cost of sweets	=	Cost of one bag	×	Number of bags bought

If one bag of sweets costs 56p, work out the total cost if Sukhvinder buys eight bags.

Cost of sweets is 56p × 8
$$= 448p$$
$$= £4.48$$

Using Letters in Formulae

Formulae can be shortened by using letters to stand for unknown amounts.

Consider the formula used in science to find the force of an object:

Force	=	Mass	×	Acceleration

This can be written as:

F	=	m	×	a

Where: F = force
 m = mass
 a = acceleration

Example
The instructions for cooking a turkey are:

'Allow 40 minutes for each kilogram of turkey, then add a further 35 minutes.'

A turkey has a mass of w kilograms. The total time to cook it is t minutes. Using letters, write a formula connecting w and t.

$t = 40w + 35$ ← Add 35 minutes.

Multiply each kilogram by 40.

Substituting into Formulae

Numbers are substituted into formulae to help solve problems.

Examples

1. The perimeter, P, of a rectangle is given by this formula:

$$P \quad = \quad 2l \quad + \quad 2w$$

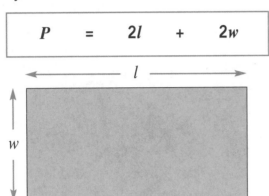

Work out the perimeter of a rectangle with $l = 6$cm and $w = 2$cm.

$P = 2l + 2w$
$\quad = 2 \times 6 + 2 \times 2$
$\quad = 12 + 4$
$\quad = 16$
So perimeter is 16cm

2. The monthly cost, C pence, of making calls from a mobile phone for m minutes is given by the following formula:

$$C \quad = \quad 450 \quad + \quad 8m$$

Work out the cost of the mobile phone bill for a month in which 80 minutes worth of calls were made.

$C = 450 + 8 \times 80$
$\quad = 450 + 640$
$\quad = 1090$
So cost is £10.90

Quick Test

1. Explain how you should write the term $b \times 3 \times a \times f$.
2. Like terms have the same letters and powers. True or false?
3. What is the expression $5a - 3b + 2a - b$ fully simplified?
   A $7a + 4b$
   B $7a - 4b$
   C $7a - 3b$
   D $5a - 6b + 2a$
4. What is multiplying out brackets also known as?
5. Multiplying out the brackets in $3(2x - 4y)$ gives $6x - 4y$. True or false?
6. $y \times y \times y \times y \times y$ written with powers is y^5. True or false?
7. How would you write the expression $2x \times 3y \times 3x$ when fully simplified?
   A $8x^2y^2$
   B $18x^2y$
   C $8x^2y$
   D $18(xy)^2$

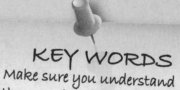

KEY WORDS
Make sure you understand these words before moving on!
- Algebra
- Term
- Coefficient
- Expression
- Like terms
- Formula
- Variable

Working with Algebra

1 In a game, Lucy has p marbles.
Write down the number of marbles that each of the following people has in terms of p.
  a) Jake has three times as many marbles as Lucy.
  b) Tia has four fewer marbles than Lucy.
  c) Hannah has six more marbles than Jake.

2 For each of the following, write out the expression that it describes:
  a) 6 less than t **f)** r less than n
  b) 5 more than h **g)** p less than y
  c) 4 more than p **h)** y more than x
  d) 2 less than m **i)** p more than m
  e) 6 more than x **j)** k less than b

3 For each of the following, write out the expression that it describes:
  a) 6 times b **e)** 3 times y
  b) a divided by 2   **f)** 2 times 5 more than x
  c) e divided by 7   **g)** p more than x, divided by y
  d) 5 times x

4 Simplify these expressions by collecting like terms:
  a) $6a + 3a - a$ **h)** $7a + 2a - b + 6b$
  b) $4b + 10b - 7b$ **i)** $2a + 7a - a$
  c) $3p + 4q - 2p + q$ **j)** $7x - 2x + 3y - y$
  d) $5x - 3y + 5y - x$ **k)** $4a - 3p + 2p - 6p + 2a$
  e) $5b + 2b$ **l)** $7b - 2b + 6b + 5b$
  f) $3a + 5b + 2a - b$ **m)** $12a - 3y - 2y - 13a + 9y$
  g) $5a - 3b + 6b$ **n)** $5p - 2p + 3p - 5a - 2a + 3b - 6b$

5 Simplify these expressions:
  a) $3x \times 2x$ **f)** $2a \times 5a$
  b) $4b \times b$ **g)** $3p \times 9p$
  c) $5b \times 3b$ **h)** $a \times 2a \times a$
  d) $4y \times 3y$ **i)** $5a \times 2a \times a$
  e) $6a \times a$ **j)** $5a \times a \times 6a$

6 Multiply out the brackets:

a) $5(x - 1)$

b) $6(x + 5)$

c) $3(2x + 4)$

d) $x(x - 6)$

e) $3(x + 1)$

f) $5(x - 4)$

g) $2(x - 6)$

h) $x(x + 5)$

i) $5(x - 6)$

j) $7(2x + 1)$

k) $x(x - 1)$

l) $3(3x - 6)$

m) $7(5 - 2x)$

n) $3x(x - 2)$

o) $6(2 - 4x)$

p) $5(3 - 6x)$

q) $2x(x - 5)$

7 If $a = 2$, $b = 3$ and $c = 5$, find the value of the following expressions:

a) $2a$

b) $5b$

c) $6c$

d) $a + 3b$

e) $5a - b$

f) $2a + 3b$

g) $6c + a$

h) $2b - 3a$

i) $5c - 2b$

j) b^2

k) $3a + 6c$

l) $10c - 2b - a$

m) $\dfrac{60}{c}$

n) $3a + \dfrac{27}{b}$

8 Billy buys some pens. He uses this formula:

Cost of pens	=	Cost of one pen	×	Number of pens bought

The cost of one pen is 28p.

Billy buys 5 pens.

Find the total price that Billy pays for the pens.

9 The temperature in Dubai is p°C.

The temperature in England is q°C.

The difference between the temperatures in Dubai and England is d°C.

Write a formula connecting d, p and q.

Equations

Solving Equations

An **equation** has two parts separated by an equals sign.

When solving an equation, a **solution** to the equation is found.

The balance method (doing the same to both sides of the equation) is often used to find the solution.

Examples
Solve the following:

1 $x + 5 = 12$

$x = 12 - 5$ ← Subtract 5 from both sides.

$x = 7$

2 $x + 25 = 20$

$x = 20 - 25$ ← Subtract 25 from both sides.

$x = -5$

3 $x - 12 = 10$

$x = 10 + 12$ ← Add 12 to both sides.

$x = 22$

4 $5x = 20$

$x = \dfrac{20}{5}$ ← Divide both sides by 5.

$x = 4$

5 $7x = 15$

$x = \dfrac{15}{7}$ ← Divide both sides by 7.

$x = 2\frac{1}{7}$

6 $\dfrac{x}{6} = 3$

$x = 3 \times 6$ ← Multiply both sides by 6.

$x = 18$

7 $\dfrac{3x}{2} = 12$

$3x = 12 \times 2$ ← Multiply both sides by 2.

$3x = 24$

$x = \dfrac{24}{3}$ ← Divide both sides by 3.

$x = 8$

Equations of the Form $ax + b = c$

Some equations are more complicated and are of the form $ax + b = c$

Examples
Solve the following:

1 $5x + 2 = 12$

$5x = 12 - 2$ ← Subtract 2 from both sides.

$5x = 10$

$x = \dfrac{10}{5}$ ← Divide both sides by 5.

$x = 2$

2 $\dfrac{x}{4} + 3 = 8$

$\dfrac{x}{4} = 8 - 3$ ← Subtract 3 from both sides.

$\dfrac{x}{4} = 5$

$x = 5 \times 4$ ← Multiply both sides by 4.

$x = 20$

3 $\dfrac{5x}{2} + 1 = 10$

$\dfrac{5x}{2} = 10 - 1$ ← Subtract 1 from both sides.

$\dfrac{5x}{2} = 9$

$5x = 9 \times 2$ ← Multiply both sides by 2.

$5x = 18$

$x = \dfrac{18}{5}$ ← Divide both sides by 5.

$x = 3\frac{3}{5}$ ← Write the answer as a mixed number.

LONSDALE

ESSENTIALS

Year 7
KS3 Mathematics
Coursebook Answers

NUMBERS

Page 6 – Quick Test

1. Nine thousand, eight hundred and thirty-two
2. Highest place value
3. a) Units
   b) Round up, because the digit is 5 or greater.

Page 7 – Skills Practice

1. a) 6 hundreds
   b) 6 units
   c) 6 units
   d) 6 hundreds
   e) 6 tens

2. a) 3 thousands
   b) 3 hundreds
   c) 3 tens
   d) 3 units
   e) 3 hundreds

3. a) 4638
   b) 605 209
   c) 83 039
   d) 9705
   e) 200 073

4. a) 7, 62, 93, 127, 156
   b) 37, 58, 201, 291, 1169
   c) 5, 18, 26, 37, 41, 52
   d) 26, 162, 583, 837, 1271

5. a) 70
   b) 70
   c) 280
   d) 1370

6. a) 700
   b) 1500
   c) 6300
   d) 3100

7. a) 5000
   b) 13 000
   c) 19 000
   d) 80 000

8. Round the numbers before adding them together.

9. No, the digits must line up according to place value, i.e.

   549
   23 –

10. a) 30 + 30 = 60
    b) 600 + 900 = 1500
    c) 80 – 20 = 60
    d) 1000 – 600 = 400

11. The shopping comes to roughly £8.50 to £8.70 so Charlie does have enough money.

12. a) 543
    b) 630
    c) 9133
    d) 486
    e) 364
    f) 1583

13. There are many possible sums that you could give. Make sure that yours has an answer of 693.

MULTIPLICATION AND DIVISION

Page 12 – Quick Test

1. Move each digit two places to the left and put two zeros at the end.

2. Move each digit three places to the right. If a number ends in zeros, up to three zeros are lost from the end.

3. The answer given when two or more numbers are multiplied together.

4. True

5. True

6. C

7. A whole number raised to the power 3 (i.e. multiplied by itself three times).

8. True

Page 13 – Skills Practice

1. a) 630
   b) 27 000
   c) 27
   d) 59
   e) 1600

2. 1095 hours

3. a) 27 full packets
   b) 2 left over

4. a) 1, 4, 5, 20
   b) 1, 4, 25, 49, 81
   c) 1, 27
   d) 6, 12, 24
   e) 3, 5, 13, 17

5. a) 15
   b) 5
   c) 5
   d) 36
   e) 64
   f) +12 or -12

6. 12 427

7. 1638

8. 17

9. a) 26
   b) 36p

FRACTIONS

Page 15 – Quick Test

1. False

2. D

3. Divide £16 by 4

4. C

5. True

Pages 16–17 – Skills Practice

1. a) i) Shaded = $\frac{7}{15}$
      ii) Not shaded = $\frac{8}{15}$
   b) i) Shaded = $\frac{1}{4}$
      ii) Not shaded = $\frac{3}{4}$
   c) i) Shaded = $\frac{5}{8}$
      ii) Not shaded = $\frac{3}{8}$

2.

3. a) $\frac{2}{3} = \frac{8}{12}$
   b) $\frac{25}{30} = \frac{5}{6}$
   c) $\frac{9}{12} = \frac{27}{36}$
   d) $\frac{20}{36} = \frac{10}{18}$

4.

   $\frac{2}{3} = \frac{10}{15}$

   $\frac{21}{27} = \frac{7}{9}$

   $\frac{4}{5} = \frac{12}{15}$

   $\frac{5}{9} = \frac{25}{45}$

5. a) 1
   b) $\frac{5}{9}$
   c) $\frac{1}{10}$
   d) $\frac{7}{16}$
   e) $\frac{21}{34}$
   f) $\frac{4}{5}$

6. $\frac{1}{6}$ of the garden is the flower bed.

7. The architect has used $\frac{1}{2}$ of the playground, so $\frac{1}{2}$ of the playground is left.

8. a) 20ml
   b) 35kg
   c) £15

9. a) 700kg
   b) £72
   c) £448

10. £6

11. a) 100 minutes
    b) 150 text messages

12. $\frac{2}{3} + \frac{4}{5}$

    $= \frac{10}{15} + \frac{12}{15}$

    $= \frac{22}{15}$

    $= 1\frac{7}{15}$, not $\frac{6}{8}$ so Jessica is wrong.

DECIMALS

Page 20 – Quick Test

1. 5 thousandths

2. True

3. B

4. 793.6

5. The number in the second decimal place.

Page 21 – Skills Practice

1. a) 3 tenths
   b) 7 hundredths
   c) 6 units
   d) 4 thousandths

2. a) 276
   b) 4.932
   c) 9630
   d) 0.2943
   e) 16 200
   f) 0.29

3. a) 518.9
   b) 260.99
   c) 114.4
   d) 42.3
   e) 171.6
   f) 45

4. a) 316.9
   b) 176.8
   c) 336.6
   d) 103.13
   e) 316.2
   f) 122

5. 4.281km

6. 0.62m

7. £7.53

8. £250.12

9. 2.41m

10. a) 6.5
    b) 7.4
    c) 5.7
    d) 4.3

11. a) 3.53
    b) 16.65
    c) 127.43
    d) 4.69
    e) 12.69
    f) 37.26
    g) 38.47
    h) 38.53
    i) 37.73

12. 1.35 metres

NEGATIVE NUMBERS

Page 23 – Quick Test

1. True

2. False

3. B

4. False

5. C

6. B

Pages 24–25 – Skills Practice

1. a) i) 7°C
      ii) -5°C
   b) i) 2°C
      ii) -6°C
   c) i) 7°C
      ii) -9°C
   d) i) 14°C
      ii) -12°C
   e) i) 13°C
      ii) -8°C
   f) i) 10°C
      ii) -9°C

2. a) -3°C, -2°C, 0°C, 4°C, 5°C, 6°C
   b) -9°C, -7°C, -2°C, 3°C, 5°C
   c) -10°C, -5°C, 2°C, 4°C, 9°C, 12°C
   d) -6°C, -4°C, -1°C, 0°C, 7°C, 9°C
   e) -12°C, -5°C, -2°C, 7°C, 9°C, 14°C
   f) -8°C, -3°C, -1°C, 6°C, 9°C, 12°C

3. a) Glasgow
   b) 7°C
   c) London
   d) Glasgow

4. 2°C

5. a) -3
   b) -5
   c) 1
   d) -9
   e) -7
   f) -10
   g) -1
   h) 4
   i) 73
   j) -5
   k) -16
   l) -7

6. a) -5, -8
   b) 1, 3
   c) -10, -12

7. a) 7
   b) 7
   c) 1
   d) 3
   e) -1
   f) -16
   g) -4
   h) -5
   i) 9
   j) 9
   k) -7
   l) 6
   m) 6
   n) -5
   o) -2

8. a)

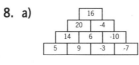

   b)

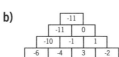

   c)

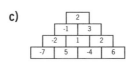

   d)

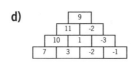

   e)

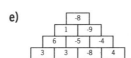

   f)

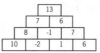

9. a)

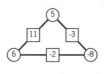

   b)

   c)

   d)

   e)

   f)

PERCENTAGES

Page 28 – Quick Test

1. %

2. Divide by 10

3. B

4. Multiply 70 by 37 and divide by 100

5. A

6. D

Page 29 – Skills Practice

1. a) 50%
   b) 25%
   c) 10%

2. 46%

3. 73%

4. 35%

5. a) 7kg
   b) £28
   c) 15mm
   d) £144
   e) £32
   f) £27
   g) £78
   h) £52.50

6. a) 102km
   b) £576
   c) 6.24kg
   d) £0.75
   e) £97.50
   f) 75.6m
   g) £29.52
   h) 224kg

7. 42 girls

8. 420 students

9. a) £33.60
   b) £593.60

10. £9.60

RATIO

Page 31 – Quick Test

1. A ratio is a way of comparing two or more related quantities.

2. True

3. D

4. B

5. Ratios are equivalent when they represent the same relationship.

Pages 32–33 – Skills Practice

1. a) 1 : 3
   b) 2 : 3
   c) 5 : 1

2. a) 1 : 2
   b) 1 : 2
   c) 2 : 5
   d) 2 : 1
   e) 15 : 7
   f) 10 : 11
   g) 4 : 3
   h) 8 : 11
   i) 5 : 11
   j) 5 : 2
   k) 16 : 1
   l) 1 : 3

3. a) 20 : 1
   b) 1 : 5
   c) 2 : 1
   d) 5 : 2
   e) 5000 : 1
   f) 4 : 1
   g) 20 : 1
   h) 1 : 4
   i) 5 : 1

4. 1 : 4

5. 1 : 2 : 5

6. 8 : 7

7. 1 : 4

8. 25 : 8 : 5

9. 13 : 9 : 15

10. £18

11. £28.21

12. £6.75

13. 5.625 tins contain enough paint for two coats, so Molly needs to buy 6 tins of paint.

14. a) £517.50
  b) £1414.50

15. a) 161.50 American dollars
  b) 389.50 American dollars

16. a) £126
  b) £226.80
  c) £302.40

17. a) 228 miles
  b) 418 miles

NUMBER PATTERNS

Page 35 – Quick Test

1. Add 3 to the preceding number.

2. The Fibonacci sequence is 1, 1, 2, 3, 5, 8, ... Each term is the sum of the previous two terms.

3. D

4. True

5. A

6. D

Pages 36–37 – Skills Practice

1. a) i) 10, 12
  ii) Add 2 each time.
  b) i) 21, 25
  ii) Add 4 each time.
  c) i) -2, -5
  ii) Subtract 3 each time.
  d) i) 4, 2
  ii) Divide by 2 each time.
  e) i) 10, 5
  ii) Subtract 5 each time.
  f) i) 45, 54
  ii) Add 9 each time.
  g) i) 30, 20
  ii) Subtract 10 each time.

h) i) 320, 640
  ii) Multiply by 2 each time.

2. a) 12, 15. Add 3 each time.
  b) 21, 25. Add 4 each time.
  c) 39, 36. Subtract 3 each time.
  d) 36, 31. Subtract 5 each time.
  e) 36, 30. Subtract 6 each time.
  f) 16, 25. Square numbers.
  g) 11, 16. Add 1, then 2, then 3, etc. That is, increase the difference by one each time.
  h) 24, 48. Multiply the previous term by 2.

3. a)

4   5

  b)

Diagram	1	2	3	4	5
No. of Squares	1	3	5	7	9

  c) 17 squares
  d) 49 squares

4. a)

  b)

Pattern	1	2	3	4
Matchsticks	3	5	7	9

  c) Add 2 each time.

5. 1, 1, 2, 3, 5, 8, 13, 21, 34, 55, 89, 144, 233, 377, 610

6. a) Add 5
  b) Subtract 2
  c) Multiply by 2
  d) Divide by 3
  e) Divide by 4
  f) Multiply by 2 and add 1

7. a) i) Input 2, 4, 6, 8
  ii) 10, 20, 30, 40
  iii) Add 10 each time / The ten times table.
  b) i) Input 2, 4, 6, 8
  ii) 8, 10, 12, 14
  iii) Add 2 each time.
  c) i) Input 2, 4, 6, 8
  ii) 7, 11, 15, 19
  iii) Add 4 each time.
  d) i) Input 2, 4, 6, 8
  ii) 4, 10, 16, 22
  iii) Add 6 each time.

8. 8, 12, 16, 20, 24, 28

9. Any four different patterns, for example:
  1, 2, 3, 4, 5, ...
  1, 2, 4, 8, 16, ...
  1, 2, 3, 5, 8, ...
  1, 2, 1, 2, 1, ...

Page 37 – Extension

Any instance of the Fibonacci sequence occurring in nature, for example: The number of petals on flowers.

WORKING WITH ALGEBRA

Page 41 – Quick Test

1. Write the number first, then the letters in alphabetical order, i.e. $3abf$.

2. True

3. B

4. Expanding brackets

5. False (the correct answer is $6x - 12y$).

6. True

7. B

Pages 42–43 – Skills Practice

1. a) $3p$
  b) $p - 4$
  c) $3p + 6$

2. a) $t - 6$
  b) $h + 5$
  c) $p + 4$
  d) $m - 2$
  e) $x + 6$
  f) $n - r$
  g) $y - p$
  h) $x + y$
  i) $m + p$
  j) $b - k$

3. a) $6b$
  b) $\frac{a}{2}$
  c) $\frac{e}{7}$
  d) $5x$
  e) $3y$
  f) $2(5 + x)$
  g) $\frac{(x + p)}{y}$

4. a) $8a$
  b) $7b$
  c) $p + 5q$
  d) $4x + 2y$
  e) $7b$
  f) $5a + 4b$

g) $5a + 3b$
  h) $9a + 5b$
  i) $8a$
  j) $5x + 2y$
  k) $6a - 7p$
  l) $16b$
  m) $4y - a$
  n) $6p - 7a - 3b$

5. a) $6x^2$
  b) $4b^2$
  c) $15b^2$
  d) $12y^2$
  e) $6a^2$
  f) $10a^2$
  g) $27p^2$
  h) $2a^3$
  i) $10a^3$
  j) $30a^3$

6. a) $5x - 5$
  b) $6x + 30$
  c) $6x + 12$
  d) $x^2 - 6x$
  e) $3x + 3$
  f) $5x - 20$
  g) $2x - 12$
  h) $x^2 + 5x$
  i) $5x - 30$
  j) $14x + 7$
  k) $x^2 - x$
  l) $9x - 18$
  m) $35 - 14x$
  n) $3x^2 - 6x$
  o) $12 - 24x$
  p) $15 - 30x$
  q) $2x^2 - 10x$

7. a) 4
  b) 15
  c) 30
  d) 11
  e) 7
  f) 13
  g) 32
  h) 0
  i) 19
  j) 9
  k) 36
  l) 42
  m) 12
  n) 15

8. £1.40

9. $d = p - q$

EQUATIONS

Page 45 – Quick Test

1. Subtract 6 from both sides of the equation.

2. Add 2 to both sides of the equation.

3. Divide both sides of the equation by 5.

4. True

5. C

Pages 46–47 – Skills Practice

1. a) $x = 4$
   b) $x = 6$
   c) $x = -3$
   d) $x = 12$
   e) $x = 3$
   f) $x = 21$
   g) $x = -1$
   h) $x = -2$
   i) $x = -5$
   j) $x = -2$
   k) $x = -3$
   l) $x = 4$
   m) $x = -5$
   n) $x = 9$

2. a) $x = 13$
   b) $x = 9$
   c) $x = 16$
   d) $x = 36$
   e) $x = 39$
   f) $x = 18$
   g) $x = 18$
   h) $x = 16$
   i) $x = 17.6$
   j) $x = 24.5$
   k) $x = 11$
   l) $x = 29$
   m) $x = 39$
   n) $x = 21$

3. a) $x = 2$
   b) $x = 3$
   c) $x = 2$
   d) $x = 3$
   e) $x = 9$
   f) $x = 8$
   g) $x = 32$
   h) $x = 8$
   i) $x = 11$
   j) $x = 2\frac{4}{7}$
   k) $x = 4\frac{4}{5}$
   l) $x = 12$
   m) $x = 4\frac{1}{3}$
   n) $x = 3\frac{1}{2}$

4. a) $x = 18$
   b) $x = 20$
   c) $x = 90$
   d) $x = 15$
   e) $x = 14$
   f) $x = 36$

5. a) $x = 9$
   b) $x = 7$
   c) $x = 10$
   d) $x = 22$
   e) $x = 15$
   f) $x = 12\frac{6}{7}$

6. a) $x = 2$
   b) $x = 11$
   c) $x = 4$
   d) $x = 8$
   e) $x = 19$
   f) $x = 9$
   g) $x = 16$
   h) $x = 6$
   i) $x = 32$
   j) $x = 30$
   k) $x = 6$
   l) $x = 2$
   m) $x = 4$
   n) $x = 13$

7. a) $x = 5$
   b) $x = 3$
   c) $x = 4$
   d) $x = 3$
   e) $x = 3$
   f) $x = 5$
   g) $x = 1$
   h) $x = 2$
   i) $x = 1$
   j) $x = 4$
   k) $x = 8$
   l) $x = 2$
   m) $x = 2\frac{2}{3}$
   n) $x = 4\frac{4}{5}$
   o) $x = 11\frac{1}{3}$

8. a) $x = 1\frac{1}{5}$
   b) $x = 2\frac{2}{3}$
   c) $x = 11\frac{1}{5}$

9. a) $9x = 288$
   $x = \frac{288}{9}$
   $x = 32$
   Raisins cost 32p

   b) $3x + 7 = 49$
   $3x = 49 - 7$
   $3x = 42$
   $x = \frac{42}{3}$
   $x = 14$

10.
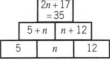
Since $2n + 17 = 35$
$2n = 35 - 17$
$2n = 18$
$n = 9$

COORDINATES AND GRAPHS

Page 49 – Quick Test

1. You read horizontally first and then vertically.

2. False

3. a) True
   b) D
   c) (-2, -4)

Pages 50–51 – Skills Practice

1. a) i)   Monkeys
      ii) Giraffes
      iii) Lions
      iv) Car park
      v)   Café
      vi) Elephants
   b) i)   (9, 3)
      ii) (2, 7)
      iii) (4, 3)

2. a) i)   Shops
      ii) Café
      iii) Church
      iv) Hotel
      v)   Fire station
   b) i)   (-7, 6)
      ii) (-7, 3)
      iii) (0, -2)
      iv) (0, -6)
      v)   (5, 2)

3. a) $x = 3$
   b) $y = 5$
   c) $x = -6$
   d) $y = -3$

4. a) 17.5 centimetres
   b) 6 inches
   c) 2.5 centimetres
   d) 4 inches

5. a)

Mass of Chicken (kg)	0.5	1.0	1.5	2.0
Cooking Time (minutes)	50	80	110	140

b)
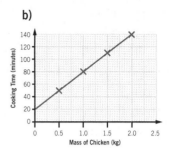

c) Approximately 95 minutes.

SHAPES

Page 54 – Quick Test

1. Lines that meet at right angles to each other.

2. Two sides are equal in length and base angles are equal.

3. True

4. 12

5. 5

Page 55 – Skills Practice

1. a)

   b) Any suitable net, for example:

   c) 8

2. a)
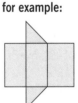

   b) Any suitable net, for example:

3. a) Any suitable net, for example:

b) 5 faces
c) 8 edges
d) 5 vertices

4. a) 1
   b) 3
   c) 1

5. a) Order 2
   b) Order 3
   c) Order 1

6. a) Parallelogram
   b) Kite

ANGLES

Page 59 – Quick Test

1. An angle greater than 180°.

2. True

3. 180°

4. 143°

5. 55°

Pages 60–61 – Skills Practice

1. a) i) Acute
      ii) 60°
   b) i) Reflex
      ii) 340°
   c) i) Obtuse
      ii) 140°
   d) i) Obtuse
      ii) 150°
   e) i) Right angle
      ii) 90°
   f) i) Acute
      ii) 65°

2. a) $a = 30°$
   b) $b = 36°$
   c) $c = 100°$

3. a) $a = 100°$
   b) $a = 155°$
   c) $a = 105°$
   d) $a = 120°$
   e) $a = 130°$, $b = 50°$, $c = 130°$
   f) $a = 56°$

4. a) $a = 60°$
   b) $a = 59°$
   c) $a = 38°$
   d) $a = 63°$
   e) $a = 70°$, $b = 55°$
   f) $a = 49°$
   g) $a = 122°$

5. a) $a = 124°$, $b = 55°$
   b) $a = 60°$, $b = 44°$
   c) $a = 82°$
   d) $a = 46°$
   e) $a = 78°$, $b = 85°$

6. Any question that gives an answer of 63°, for example: A triangle has one angle measuring 42°, another angle measuring 75°, what is the size of the third angle?

7. a)–b) Accurate diagrams constructed using the given measurements.
   Lengths should be drawn correctly to within ±1mm. Angles should be drawn correctly to within ±1°.

MEASURES AND MEASUREMENT

Page 65 – Quick Test

1. True

2. D

3. True

4. False

5. B

6. C

Pages 66–67 – Skills Practice

1. a) Centimetres
   b) Kilometres
   c) Millimetres
   d) Grams
   e) Tonnes
   f) Grams

2. a) 6.2kg
   b) 720mm
   c) 61 000cm
   d) 5000kg
   e) 300cl
   f) 6200m
   g) 16 300g
   h) 72.5cm
   i) 9.6cl
   j) 5.2cm
   k) 8.6cl
   l) 3.6kg
   m) 0.525kg
   n) 1.06l
   o) 7.2km
   p) 6300g
   q) 0.56m
   r) 7200ml
   s) 2700g

3. 8 times

4. a) 1507cm
   b) 15.07m

5. 1m 62cm, 1m 640mm, 3m 25cm, 562cm, 5700mm

6. Yes, it can all go in the lift at once (the total weight is 283kg).

7. a) 0720
   b) 1915
   c) 2036
   d) 1025

8. a) 9.16am
   b) 10.18pm
   c) 5.32pm
   d) 4.25am

9. a) 47 minutes
   b) 54 minutes
   c) 35 minutes
   d) 126 minutes
   e) 132 minutes
   f) 79 minutes
   g) 4 minutes
   h) 56 minutes

10. 8.25am

11. 105 minutes (or 1 hour 45 minutes).

12. 12.5 miles

13. 14.4 litres

PERIMETER, AREA AND VOLUME

Page 71 – Quick Test

1. The distance around the outside edge of a shape.

2. A

3. C

4. False

5. D

Pages 72–73 – Skills Practice

1. a) 10cm
   b) 22cm

2. a) 6cm^2
   b) 19cm^2

3. Any shape with a perimeter of 20cm, for example: An 8 × 2 rectangle.

4. Approximately 14cm^2

5. a) 12cm^2
   b) 36cm^2

c) 42cm^2
d) 100cm^2
e) 28cm^2
f) 82.96cm^2

6. a) 156cm
   b) 1512cm^2

7. a) 20cm^2
   b) 27cm^2
   c) 8.7cm^2
   d) 42cm^2
   e) 45cm^2
   f) 12.24cm^2

8. 8200m^2

9. a) 24cm^3
   b) 40cm^3
   c) 40cm^3
   d) 350cm^3
   e) 288cm^3

HANDLING DATA

Page 77 – Quick Test

1. a) By questionnaire / survey.
   b) Primary
   c) Discrete
   d) A tally chart. The data is unlikely to cover a wide range of values, so this is a better choice than a frequency table.
   e) Pictogram, bar chart or bar line graph.

2. A tally chart records each piece of data as an individual mark, while a frequency table records the total number of data items as a number.

3. a) The newsagent sells at least 250 cards every month, with high sales in November, December and February. There are low sales in January, May, July and September.
   b) The peaks on the graph correspond to occasions when lots of people might buy cards – Valentine's Day in February and Christmas in November / December. There were also smaller rises in March, April and June, which could be due to Mother's Day, Easter and Father's Day.

Pages 78–79 – Skills Practice

1.

Type of Book	Tally	Frequency
Fiction		
Non-fiction		
Horror		
Autobiography		
Other		

2. The first two options overlap. Those who receive £1 could tick both boxes.

3. a)

Sport	Tally	Frequency
Swimming	⦀⦀ I	6
Squash	⦀⦀	5
Badminton	III	3
Yoga	⦀⦀ I	6

b)

Choice of Sport

Swimming	♦♦♦♦♦♦
Squash	♦♦♦♦♦
Badminton	♦♦♦
Yoga	♦♦♦♦♦♦

Key ♦ represents 1 person

c)

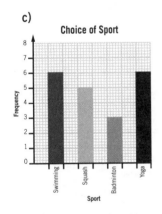

Choice of Sport

d) Swimming and yoga

4. a) Coffee
   b) 140
   c) **Any suitable answer, for example:** The flavour of the soup might not have appealed to customers.

5. a) 10
   b) 2

c) **Any suitable answer, for example:** Most students might live close to school or the school might have a healthy lifestyle policy.

6. a) **Any suitable answer, for example:** The weather was hot and sunny or the café might have only opened for half of the day.
   b) **Any suitable answer, for example:** The weather was cold or the café had more customers because more people go out on a weekend.

AVERAGES

Page 82 – Quick Test

1. The mode is the number that occurs most often.

2. False (the correct answer is 8).

3. B

4. C

5.

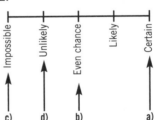

$$\text{Mean} = \frac{\text{Sum of a set of values}}{\text{The number of values in the set}}$$

Page 83 – Skills Practice

1. a) 6.2
   b) 7
   c) 7
   d) 6

2. a) 6
   b) 5.5
   c) 3
   d) 8

3. a) 5.06
   b) 4.75
   c) 4.7
   d) 6.7

4. 7K got the highest mean mark. There was also less spread in their data, so 7K did the best in general. 7M, however, did have some students who scored higher than the highest scoring student in 7K.

5. Mean = 2.4 experiments (to 1 d.p.)

6. a) 1.25
   b) 1
   c) 3

PROBABILITY

Page 86 – Quick Test

1. Probability is the chance that something will happen.

2. a) C
   b) A
   c) B

3. True

4. True

Page 87 – Skills Practice

1. a) Impossible
   b) Certain (unless birthday is on 29th February)
   c) Impossible
   d) Possible

2.

Impossible — Unlikely — Even chance — Likely — Certain

c)   d)   b)   a)

3. **Any suitable outcomes, for example:**
   A – A person has five heads.
   B – Winning the lottery jackpot.
   C – Getting a head when a coin is thrown.
   D – The Sun rises in the East (unless at North or South pole).

4. a) Red, Yellow, Pink, Black, Blue, Green
   b) Red, Pink, Blue, Green, Orange

5. a) $\frac{3}{9} = \frac{1}{3}$
   b) 0
   c) $\frac{4}{9}$

6. a) $\frac{2}{11}$
   b) $\frac{4}{11}$
   c) $\frac{1}{11}$
   d) 0

ACKNOWLEDGEMENTS

The author and publisher are grateful to the copyright holders for permission to use quoted materials and images.

All other images © 2008 Jupiterimages Corporation, and Lonsdale

Every effort has been made to trace copyright holders and obtain their permission for the use of copyright material. The author and publisher will gladly receive information enabling them to rectify any error or omission in subsequent editions. All facts are correct at time of going to press.

Published by Lonsdale
An imprint of HarperCollins*Publishers*
77–85 Fulham Palace Road
London W6 8JB

© 2008, 2011 Lonsdale

ISBN: 978-1905896-66-0

First published 2008

02/040211

British Library Cataloguing in Publication Data.

A CIP record of this book is available from the British Library.

Book concept and development: Helen Jacobs and Rebecca Skinner
Author: Fiona Mapp
Project Editor: David Mantovani
Cover Design: Angela English
Inside Concept Design: Helen Jacobs and Sarah Duxbury
Text Design and Layout: Anne-Marie Taylor
Artwork: Lonsdale
Printed in the UK

Using Equations to Solve Word Problems

When solving problems, an equation can be written to find an unknown value.

Examples

1 The perimeter of the triangle is 32cm.

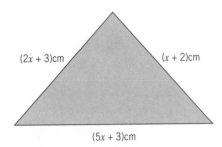

(2x + 3)cm   (x + 2)cm

(5x + 3)cm

a) Write down an equation for the perimeter.

The equation is...
$2x + 3 + x + 2 + 5x + 3 = 32$

Collecting like terms gives $8x + 8 = 32$

b) Solve the equation.

$$8x + 8 = 32$$
$$8x = 32 - 8$$
$$8x = 24$$
$$x = \frac{24}{8}$$
$$x = 3$$

c) Write down the length of each side of the triangle.

Substitute $x = 3$ into each expression to find the lengths of the triangle:

$$2x + 3 = 2 \times 3 + 3$$
$$= 9$$

$$x + 2 = 3 + 2$$
$$= 5$$

$$5x + 3 = 5 \times 3 + 3$$
$$= 18$$

So the sides are 9cm, 5cm and 18cm.

2 The cost of hiring a van is £15 per hour, plus £45. Mr Jones hires a van for x hours and pays a total of £135.
Write an equation and solve it to find out how many hours Mr Jones hired the van for.

$$15x + 45 = 135$$

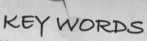

£15 per hour.   Standing charge of £45.

$$15x = 135 - 45$$
$$15x = 90$$
$$x = \frac{90}{15}$$
$$x = 6$$

Mr Jones hired the van for 6 hours.

Quick Test

1. Explain how you would solve the equation
   $x + 6 = 10$
2. Explain how you would solve the equation
   $x - 2 = 12$
3. Explain how you would solve the equation
   $5x = 20$
4. The solution to the equation $5x + 2 = 17$ is $x = 3$.
   True or false?
5. What is the solution to the equation
   $\frac{x}{2} + 1 = 5$?

   A 12   **B** 3   **C** 8   **D** 10

Equations

1 Solve the following:

a) $x + 2 = 6$

b) $x + 3 = 9$

c) $x + 10 = 7$

d) $x + 12 = 24$

e) $x + 9 = 12$

f) $x + 6 = 27$

g) $x + 10 = 9$

h) $x + 6 = 4$

i) $x + 10 = 5$

j) $x + 9 = 7$

k) $x + 15 = 12$

l) $5 + x = 9$

m) $7 + x = 2$

n) $10 + x = 19$

2 Solve the following:

a) $x - 4 = 9$

b) $x - 7 = 2$

c) $x - 10 = 6$

d) $x - 9 = 27$

e) $x - 8 = 31$

f) $15 = x - 3$

g) $x - 6 = 12$

h) $x - 9 = 7$

i) $x - 5 = 12.6$

j) $x - 9 = 15.5$

k) $7 = x - 4$

l) $26 = x - 3$

m) $38 = x - 1$

n) $15 = x - 6$

3 Solve the following:

a) $5x = 10$

b) $6x = 18$

c) $3x = 6$

d) $9x = 27$

e) $9x = 81$

f) $7x = 56$

g) $2x = 64$

h) $8x = 64$

i) $5x = 55$

j) $7x = 18$

k) $5x = 24$

l) $12x = 144$

m) $3x = 13$

n) $2x = 7$

4 Solve the following:

a) $\dfrac{x}{3} = 6$

b) $\dfrac{x}{2} = 10$

c) $\dfrac{x}{9} = 10$

d) $5 = \dfrac{x}{3}$

e) $\dfrac{x}{7} = 2$

f) $9 = \dfrac{x}{4}$

5 Solve the following:

a) $\dfrac{2x}{3} = 6$

b) $\dfrac{5x}{7} = 5$

c) $\dfrac{4x}{5} = 8$

d) $\dfrac{6x}{11} = 12$

e) $\dfrac{3x}{5} = 9$

f) $\dfrac{7x}{9} = 10$

6 Solve the following:

a) $x + 4 = 6$

b) $x - 2 = 9$

c) $x + 6 = 10$

d) $x - 5 = 3$

e) $x - 7 = 12$

f) $x + 2 = 11$

g) $x - 6 = 10$

h) $\dfrac{x}{3} = 2$

i) $\dfrac{x}{4} = 8$

j) $\dfrac{x}{5} = 6$

k) $5x = 30$

l) $6x = 12$

m) $7x = 28$

n) $10x = 130$

7 Solve the following:

a) $2x + 1 = 11$

b) $3x - 2 = 7$

c) $5x + 1 = 21$

d) $4x - 2 = 10$

e) $7x - 1 = 20$

f) $10x + 5 = 55$

g) $4x + 6 = 10$

h) $7x - 2 = 12$

i) $9x - 1 = 8$

j) $5x + 3 = 23$

k) $5x - 4 = 36$

l) $7x + 6 = 20$

m) $3x - 2 = 6$

n) $5x - 4 = 20$

o) $3x + 2 = 36$

8 Solve the following:

a) $\dfrac{5x}{2} + 6 = 9$

b) $\dfrac{3x}{2} + 8 = 12$

c) $\dfrac{5x}{7} + 2 = 10$

9 For each of the following, write an equation to solve the problem.

a) Rachael buys 9 bags of raisins.
The total cost is £2.88
How much does each bag of raisins cost?

b) David thinks of a number.
He multiplies it by 3 and adds 7.
His answer is 49.
What number did he think of?

10 Look at the following number pyramid:

35	
5	n	12

The number in each cell is the sum of the
two cells beneath it.
Copy and complete the number pyramid and
use the information to find the value of n.

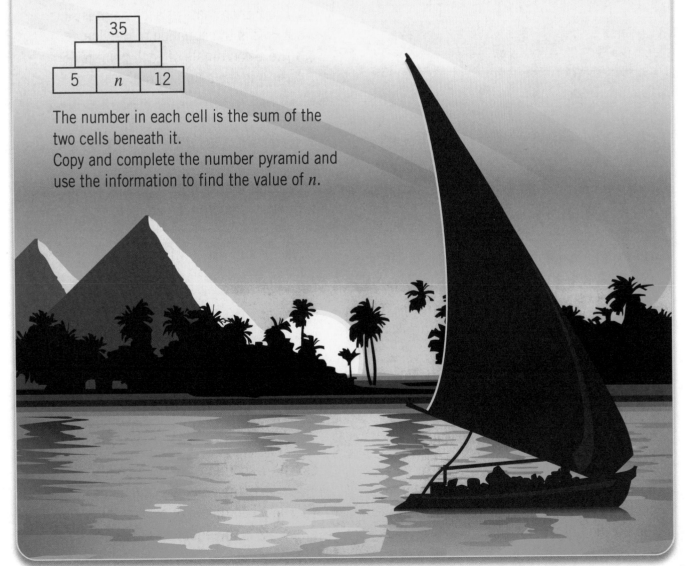

Coordinates and Graphs

Coordinates

Coordinates are used to locate the position of a point.

When reading coordinates, you read horizontally first (the x-coordinate) and then vertically (the y-coordinate).

The **horizontal** axis is the x-**axis**.

The **vertical** axis is the y-**axis**.

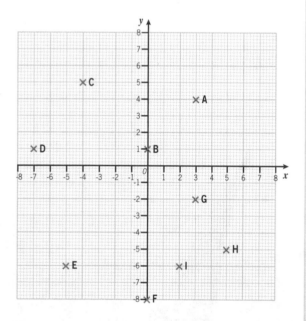

On the above graph, the coordinates of the points, A to I, are...

A	(3, 4)	F	(0, -8)
B	(0, 1)	G	(3, -2)
C	(-4, 5)	H	(5, -5)
D	(-7, 1)	I	(2, -6)
E	(-5, -6)		

Coordinates are always written in brackets with a comma between the two values, for example, (3, 4).

In geography, grid references are similar to coordinates in that they help you to locate the position of a point.

Graphs of the Form $x = a$

A graph of the form $x = a$ is a vertical line with every x-coordinate equal to a.

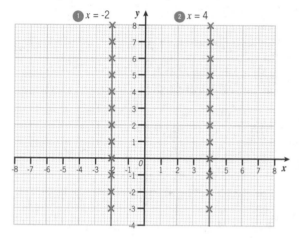

1. The x-coordinate of each point is -2.
   $x = -2$ is the equation of the line.
2. The x-coordinate of each point is 4.
   $x = 4$ is the equation of the line.

Graphs of the Form $y = b$

A graph of the form $y = b$ is a horizontal line with every y-coordinate equal to b.

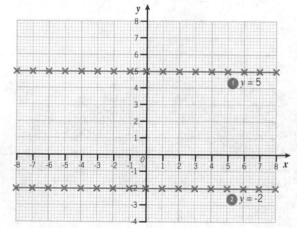

1. The y-coordinate of each point is 5.
   $y = 5$ is the equation of the line.
2. The y-coordinate of each point is -2.
   $y = -2$ is the equation of the line.

Interpreting Graphs

Linear graphs are often used to show relationships.

For example, a hire firm charges £25 per hour to rent a van, plus a standing charge of £50. Using this information, you can work out the first few values and draw up a table:

Number of Hours	1	2	3	4	5
Charge (£)	75	100	125	150	175

You can now plot this information on a graph.

Plotting the points shows a linear relationship between the rental time and the charge.
The graph can be used to find, for example, how long a van is hired for if the charge is £200, in this case 6 hours.

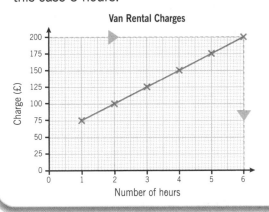

Conversion Graphs

Conversion graphs are used to change one unit of measurement into another unit, for example, kilometres to miles or £ to €.

For example, the graph below shows the conversion rate between GB pounds and US dollars (£1 = $2.10).

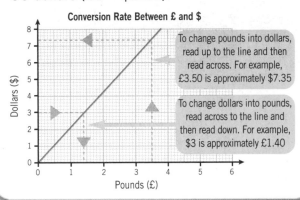

To change pounds into dollars, read up to the line and then read across. For example, £3.50 is approximately $7.35

To change dollars into pounds, read across to the line and then read down. For example, $3 is approximately £1.40

Quick Test

1 Explain how you read coordinates.
2 The horizontal axis is called the *y*-axis. True or false?
3 Use the coordinate grid to answer the following questions:

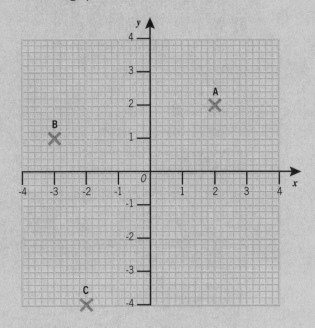

a) The coordinates of A are (2, 2). True or false?

b) The coordinates of B are…
   A (3, 1)
   B (1, -3)
   C (-1, 3)
   D (-3, 1)

c) What are the coordinates of C?

KEY WORDS
Make sure you understand these words before moving on!
- Coordinates
- Horizontal
- Vertical
- x-axis
- y-axis
- Linear
- Conversion

49

Coordinates and Graphs

1. Look at this map of a zoo.
   a) What can be found at each of the following coordinates?
      i) (4, 1)
      ii) (7, 5)
      iii) (7, 8)
      iv) (1, 4)
      v) (10, 1)
      vi) (9, 6)
   b) What are the coordinates of…
      i) the gift shop?
      ii) the sea lions?
      iii) the toilets?

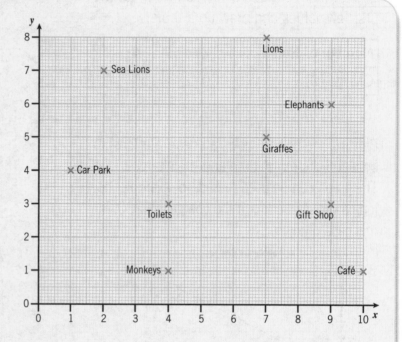

2. The following grid shows the map of an island.
   a) What is at each of the following coordinates?
      i) (3, 4)
      ii) (-4, 2)
      iii) (-4, -6)
      iv) (7, -5)
      v) (4, -2)
   b) From the map, what are the coordinates of the…
      i) lighthouse?
      ii) hostel?
      iii) hospital?
      iv) police station?
      v) farm?

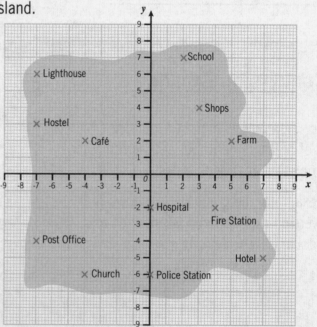

3 From the grid opposite, write down the equation of...
   a) line A
   b) line B
   c) line C
   d) line D

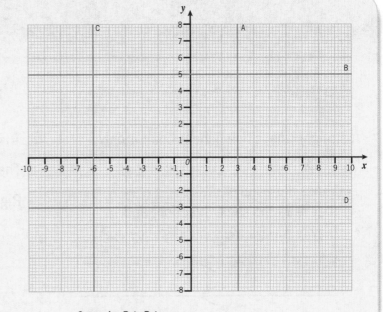

4 The following graph shows the relationship between inches and centimetres.

Use the graph to convert...
   a) 7 inches into centimetres
   b) 15 centimetres into inches
   c) 1 inch into centimetres
   d) 10 centimetres into inches.

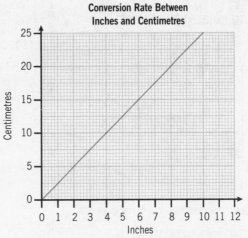

Conversion Rate Between Inches and Centimetres

5 A cookery book gives these instructions for roasting a chicken:

Cook for 30 minutes per $\frac{1}{2}$ kilogram (500 grams), plus 20 minutes.

a) Copy and complete the table.

Mass of Chicken (kg)	0.5	1.0	1.5	2.0
Cooking Time (minutes)		80		

b) Copy the following axes onto graph paper. On your axes, plot the values from the table you completed in part a).

c) Use your graph to estimate the cooking time for a chicken with a mass of 1.25kg.

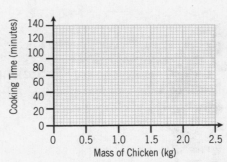

Shapes

Lines

A straight line is one-dimensional; it only has length.

Two lines are **parallel** if...
- they're in the same direction, and
- they're always the same distance apart.

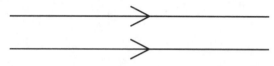

Two lines are **perpendicular** if they're at right angles to each other.

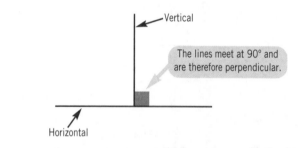

Vertical

The lines meet at 90° and are therefore perpendicular.

Horizontal

Two-Dimensional Shapes

Two-dimensional shapes have area. They are usually referred to as 2-D shapes.

You need to be able to recognise the 2-D shapes given on these pages, along with some of their important features.

Islamic art is often made up of two-dimensional shapes:

Triangles

Triangles have three sides.

There are several types of triangle:

Right-angled
- Has a 90° angle.

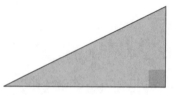

Isosceles
- Two sides are equal.
- Base angles are equal.

Equilateral
- Three sides are equal.
- Three angles are equal (60°).

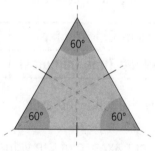

Scalene
- All the sides and angles are different.

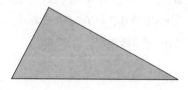

Quadrilaterals

Quadrilaterals have four sides.

There are several types of quadrilateral:

Square
- All angles are 90°.
- All sides are equal.
- Four lines of symmetry.
- Rotational symmetry of order 4.

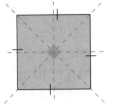

Rectangle
- All angles are 90°.
- Opposite sides are equal.
- Two lines of symmetry.
- Rotational symmetry of order 2.

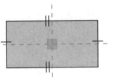

Parallelogram
- No lines of symmetry.
- Rotational symmetry of order 2.
- Opposite sides are parallel and equal in length.
- Opposite angles are equal.

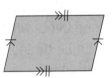

Rhombus
- Two lines of symmetry.
- Rotational symmetry of order 2.
- All sides are equal in length.
- Opposite sides are parallel.
- Opposite angles are equal.

Kite
- One line of symmetry.
- No rotational symmetry.
- Has two pairs of adjacent sides equal in length.

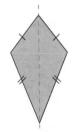

Trapezium
- One pair of parallel sides.
- No lines of symmetry unless it's an isosceles trapezium.
- No rotational symmetry.
- Non-parallel sides equal in length (isosceles trapezium only).

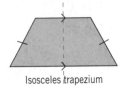

Isosceles trapezium

Three-Dimensional Solids

Three-dimensional (3-D) objects have volume (or 'capacity').

Here are some of the 3-D solids that you should know:

Cube

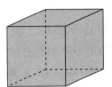

Cuboid

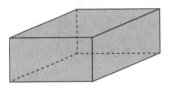

Sphere

Cylinder

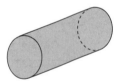

Cone

Triangular prism

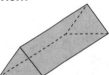

Square-based pyramid

Shapes

3-D Solids and Nets

- A **prism** is a solid that can be cut into slices that are all the same shape.
- A **face** is a flat surface of a solid.
- An **edge** is where two faces meet.
- **Vertex** is another word for 'corner'. The plural of vertex is **vertices**.

For example, a cube has: 6 faces
8 vertices
12 edges

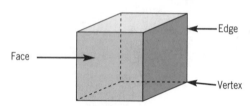

A **net** of a 3-D solid is a 2-D (flat) shape that can be folded to make the 3-D solid.

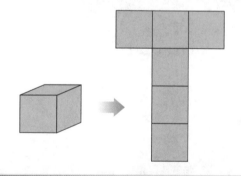

Symmetry

Reflective symmetry – this is when both sides of a shape are the same on each side of a **mirror line**. The mirror line is known as a **line**, or **axis**, **of symmetry**.

2 lines of symmetry

1 line of symmetry

Rotational symmetry – a 2-D shape has rotational symmetry if it can be turned to look exactly the same. The order of rotational symmetry is the number of times the shape can be turned and still look the same.

Order 4

Plane symmetry – a 3-D solid has a plane of symmetry if the plane divides the shape into two halves and one half is the exact mirror image of the other. 3-D solids can have more than one plane of symmetry.

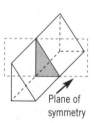

Plane of symmetry

Quick Test

1. Explain what perpendicular lines are.
2. What are the properties of an isosceles triangle?
3. A parallelogram has rotational symmetry of order 2. True or false?
4. How many edges does a cuboid have?
5. How many faces does a triangular prism have?

Skills Practice

1 a) Sketch a copy of this cuboid:

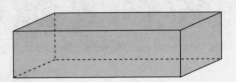

On your sketch, draw in a plane of symmetry.
b) Sketch the net of the cuboid.
c) How many vertices does the cuboid have?

2 A chocolate bar is packaged in a triangular prism.

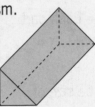

a) Sketch a copy of the prism and mark in the plane of symmetry.
b) Sketch the net of the chocolate bar's packaging.

3 a) Draw the net of this square-based pyramid.

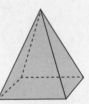

b) How many faces does the square-based pyramid have?
c) How many edges does the square-based pyramid have?
d) How many vertices does the square-based pyramid have?

4 How many lines of symmetry does each of the following shapes have?

a)

b)

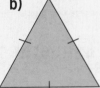

c)

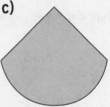

5 What is the order of rotational symmetry of each of these shapes?

a)

b)

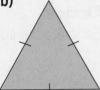

c)

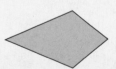

6 What quadrilaterals are being described?
a) I have no lines of symmetry and rotational symmetry of order two.
My opposite sides are equal in length and parallel.
My opposite angles are equal.
b) I have one line of symmetry, but no rotational symmetry.
My diagonals cross at right angles, but they don't bisect each other.
I have two pairs of adjacent sides that are equal.

Angles

Angles

An angle is an amount of turning or rotation.

Angles are measured in **degrees**.

A circle is divided into 360 parts. Each part is called a degree and is represented by a small circle °.

A protractor is used to measure the size of an angle.

Always put 0° at the start position and then read from the correct scale.

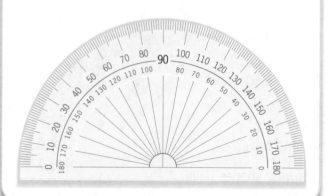

Types of Angle

- An **acute angle** is between 0° and 90°.

- An **obtuse angle** is between 90° and 180°.

- A **reflex angle** is between 180° and 360°.

- A **right angle** is 90°.

Reading Angles

When asked to find angle ABC, or AB̂C, or ∠ABC, the angle you are finding is the middle letter. In this case, angle B.

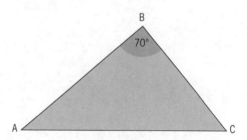

In the above triangle, angle ABC = 70°.

Estimating Angles

To estimate the size of an angle, it's useful to compare it to the size of a right angle.

Example
Estimate the size of this angle.

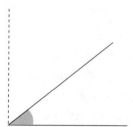

Comparing the angle to a right angle, it's just under half the size, so it's approximately 40°.

Angles not drawn to scale

Angles on a Straight Line

The angles on a straight line add up to 180°.

$a + b + c = 180°$

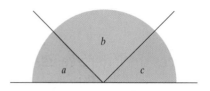

Example
Work out the size of angle x.

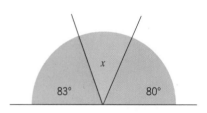

$$83° + 80° + x = 180°$$
$$163° + x = 180°$$
$$x = 180° - 163°$$
$$x = 17°$$

Angles at a Point

The angles at a point add up to 360°.

$a + b + c = 360°$

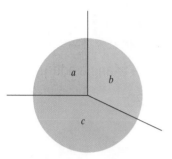

Example
Work out the size of angle y.

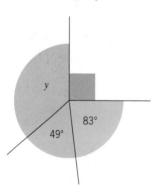

$$y + 90° + 83° + 49° = 360°$$
$$y + 222° = 360°$$
$$y = 360° - 222°$$
$$y = 138°$$

Vertically Opposite Angles

Vertically opposite angles are formed when two straight lines intersect (cross).

Vertically opposite angles are equal:
- a and c are opposite each other, so $a = c$.
- b and d are opposite each other, so $b = d$.

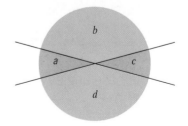

Example
Work out the missing angles.

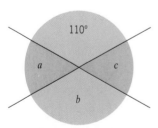

$$a = 180° - 110° = 70°$$
$$b = 110°$$
$$c = 70°$$

Angles

Angles in a Triangle

The angles in a triangle add up to 180°.

$a + b + c = 180°$

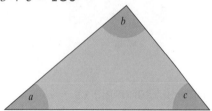

Any exterior angle of a triangle is equal to the sum of the two opposite interior angles.

$a + b = c$

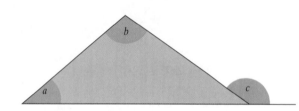

Examples

What angles does the letter a represent?

 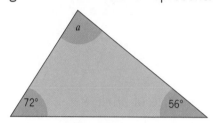

$a + 72° + 56° = 180°$
$a + 128° = 180°$
$a = 180° - 128°$
$a = 52°$

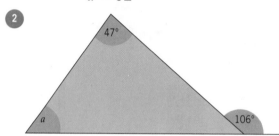

$a + 47° = 106°$
$a = 106° - 47°$
$a = 59°$

Angles in an Isosceles Triangle

Examples

1 Find the missing angles in this isosceles triangle.

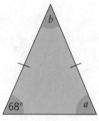

$a = 68°$ since the base angles are equal.
$b + 68° + 68° = 180°$
$b = 180° - 136°$
$b = 44°$

2 Find the missing angles in this isosceles triangle.

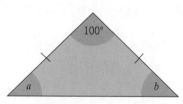

$a = b$ since the base angles are equal.
$2a = 180° - 100°$
$2a = 80°$
$a = 40° = b$

Angles not drawn to scale

Angles in a Quadrilateral

The angles in a quadrilateral add up to 360°.

$a + b + c + d = 360°$

Example
Find the missing angle, a.

$$a + 75° + 122° + 107° = 360°$$
$$a = 360° - 304°$$
$$a = 56°$$

Constructing Triangles

Triangular shapes are often used in designs for bridges, fun fair rides, etc. because they are strong.

It's important that architects and engineers draw their diagrams accurately. An accurate drawing is called a **construction**.

Example
Construct this triangle:

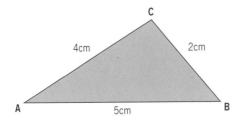

Follow these steps to construct the triangle:
1. Draw the longest side, i.e. AB.
2. With the compass point at A, draw an arc of radius 4cm.
3. With the compass point at B, draw an arc of radius 2cm.
4. Join A and B to the point where the two arcs meet.

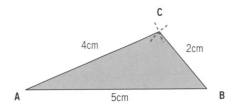

You can also construct triangles if you're given the angles. You must measure and draw the angles very carefully.

Quick Test

1. Explain what a reflex angle is.
2. An acute angle lies between 0° and 90°. True or false?
3. What do the angles on a straight line add up to?
4. Two angles meet at a point. One of the angles is 217°. What is the size of the other angle?
5. Three angles in a quadrilateral add up to 305°. What is the size of the fourth angle?

KEY WORDS
Make sure you understand these words before moving on!
- Degree
- Acute angle
- Obtuse angle
- Reflex angle
- Right angle
- Construction

Angles

Skills Practice

1 For each of the angles below...
    i) write down the type of angle
    ii) estimate its size.

a)

c)

e)

b)

d)

f)

2 Work out the size of the missing angles.

a)

b)

c)

3 Work out the size of the missing angles.

a)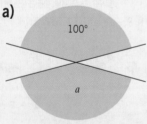

c)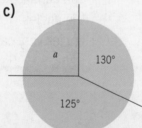

e)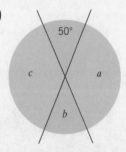

b)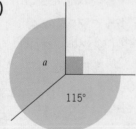

d)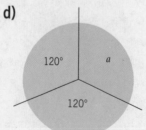

f)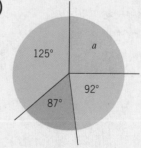

Angles not drawn to scale

4 Work out the size of the missing angles.

a)

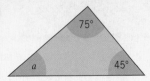

b)

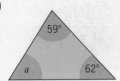

c)

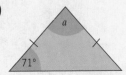

d)

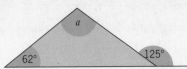

e)

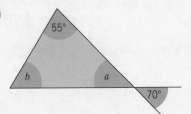

f)

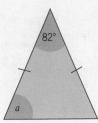

g)

5 Work out the size of the missing angles.

a)

b)

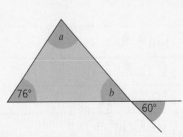

c)

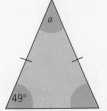

d)

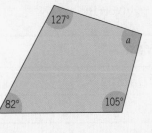

e)

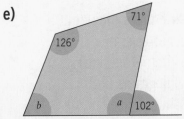

6 The answer to an angle question is 63°.
Write down a question for which the answer is an angle of 63°.

7 Construct these triangles:

a)

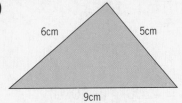

b)

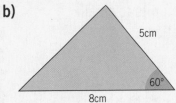

Measures and Measurement

Estimating

Estimating is a useful skill in everyday life. Some of the measurements that you might need to estimate are given below:

- Length – for example, an average swimming pool is about 25m long.
- Mass – for example, a bag of sugar has a mass of about 1kg.
- Capacity – for example, a can of soft drink holds about 330ml, or about half a pint.
- Time – for example, it takes approximately $2\frac{1}{2}$ hours to travel from Manchester to London by train.

Metric Units

Metric units include...
- metres (m)
- kilometres (km)
- kilograms (kg)
- litres (l)
- centilitres (cl).

The table below shows the metric equivalents.

Length	Mass	Capacity
10mm = 1cm	1000mg = 1g	1000ml = 1l
100cm = 1m	1000g = 1kg	100cl = 1l
1000m = 1km	1000kg = 1 tonne	1000cm³ = 1l

When converting units, remember...
- to change from small units to large units, use division
- to change from large units to small units, use multiplication.

Examples

1. 600m = 0.6km (÷ 1000)
2. 3500g = 3.5kg (÷ 1000)
3. 37mm = 3.7cm (÷ 10)
4. 96cm = 960mm (× 10)
5. 5kg = 5000g (× 1000)
6. 7l = 700cl (× 100)
7. 4.2 tonnes = 4200kg (× 1000)

Imperial Units

Imperial units include…
- miles
- yards
- stones
- pounds (lb)
- ounces (oz).

Imperial units are sometimes thought of as old fashioned units of measurement.

The table below shows the imperial equivalents.

Since January 2000, traders have had to weigh and sell loose items, such as fruit and vegetables, in metric units, such as grams and kilograms, rather than imperial measures.

However, there has been opposition from traders and shoppers who still prefer imperial units.

Imperial units can currently be displayed alongside metric units, as long as they are not larger than the metric units.

Length	Mass	Capacity
1 foot = 12 inches	1 stone = 14 pounds	20 fluid oz = 1 pint
1 yard = 3 feet	1 pound = 16 ounces	8 pints = 1 gallon

Converting between Metric and Imperial

This table shows some approximate comparisons between metric and imperial units:

Length	Mass	Capacity
2.5cm ≈ 1 inch	25g ≈ 1 ounce	$1l ≈ 1\frac{3}{4}$ pints
30cm ≈ 1 foot	1kg ≈ 2.2 pounds	4.5l ≈ 1 gallon
1m ≈ 39 inches		
8km ≈ 5 miles		

Examples

1 Change 30km into miles.

8km = 5 miles
So $1km = \frac{5}{8}$ mile

$30km = 30 \times \frac{5}{8}$ mile
$\qquad = 18.75$ miles (to 2 d.p.)

2 Mr Roberts buys 500g of apples.
Approximately how many pounds is this?

$500g = \frac{1}{2}kg$
1kg = 2.2 pounds

So 500g = 1.1 pounds

Measures and Measurement

Choosing the Correct Units of Measurement

The following examples show the units that you should use to measure some everyday quantities.

1 Length
- Thickness of a book (mm).
- Width of a door (cm).
- Height of a house (m).
- Distance from Leeds to Newcastle (km).

2 Mass
- A packet of sweets (g).
- A bag of flour (kg).
- A car (tonnes).

3 Capacity
- A spoonful of gravy powder (ml).
- A bottle of juice (cl).
- The amount of water in a pond (l).

Time

The 12-hour clock uses am and pm:
- Times before midday are am.
- Times after midday are pm.

The 24-hour clock numbers the hours from 0 to 24. Times are written with four figures.

The numbers on the outside show a 12-hour clock and the first 12 hours of a 24-hour clock. The numbers on the inside show the last 12 hours of a 24-hour clock.

From the above clock you can see that...
- 3.47pm is the same as 1547
- 2.30am is the same as 0230.

There are...
- 60 seconds in 1 minute
- 60 minutes in 1 hour
- 24 hours in 1 day
- 7 days in 1 week
- 52 weeks in 1 year.

Example
Josh set off for work at 8.10am and arrived at 9.05am. How long did it take Josh to get to work?

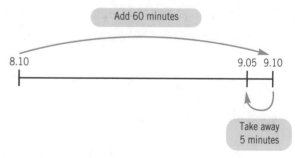

Total time = 55 minutes.

Reading Scales

It's important that you can read the scales on a range of instruments and objects. Some common examples are shown below.

Weighing scales

The bag of flour on this scale shows 450g.

Measuring cylinder

This cylinder shows 400ml of water.

Jug

This jug contains 75cl of water.

Ruler

This ruler shows 12cm.

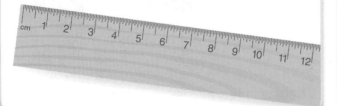

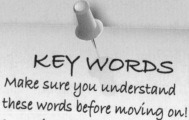

KEY WORDS
Make sure you understand these words before moving on!
• Metric units
• Imperial units

Measures and Measurement

1. What metric units would you measure each of these objects in?
   a) Length of a pen.
   b) Length of the M6 motorway.
   c) Thickness of a coin.
   d) Mass of a textbook.
   e) Mass of a bus.
   f) Mass of a fork.

2. Change each of the following quantities into the units given in brackets.
   a) 6200g (kg)
   b) 72cm (mm)
   c) 610m (cm)
   d) 5 tonnes (kg)
   e) 3 litres (cl)
   f) 6.2km (m)
   g) 16.3kg (g)
   h) 725mm (cm)
   i) 96ml (cl)
   j) 52mm (cm)
   k) 86ml (cl)
   l) 3600g (kg)
   m) 525g (kg)
   n) 106cl (l)
   o) 7200m (km)
   p) 6.3kg (g)
   q) 56cm (m)
   r) 7.2 litres (ml)
   s) 2.7kg (g)

3. A glass holds 25cl of liquid when full.
   How many times can it be filled from a two-litre bottle?

4. Add together these lengths:

   65cm, 2m, 345cm, 3m 62cm, 5m 35cm

   Give the total in...
   a) centimetres
   b) metres.

5. Put these lengths in order of size:

   562cm, 3m 25cm, 1m 62cm, 5700mm, 1m 640mm

6. A lift can carry a maximum mass of 300kg.
   The masses of some furniture are as follows:

Sofa 105kg

Chair 16kg

Dresser 93kg

Can all the furniture go into the lift at once, plus Bob, who has a mass of 69kg?

7 Change each of the following to 24-hour clock time.

  a) 7.20am   **c)** 8.36pm

  b) 7.15pm   **d)** 10.25am

8 Change each of the following to 12-hour clock time.

  a) 0916   **c)** 1732

  b) 2218   **d)** 0425

9 Work out how many minutes there are between the following pairs of times:

  a) 0800 and 0847   **e)** 0016 and 0228

  b) 0926 and 1020   **f)** 1407 and 1526

  c) 1251 and 1326   **g)** 1619 and 1623

  d) 1521 and 1727   **h)** 2214 and 2310

10 It takes Katie 25 minutes to walk to school.

  What time must she leave home in order to arrive at school by 8.50am?

11 Reece spends 25 minutes doing maths homework, 38 minutes doing English homework and 42 minutes doing piano practice.

  How long did Reece spend in total doing his homework and piano practice?

12 Change 20km into miles.

13 Change 3.2 gallons into litres.

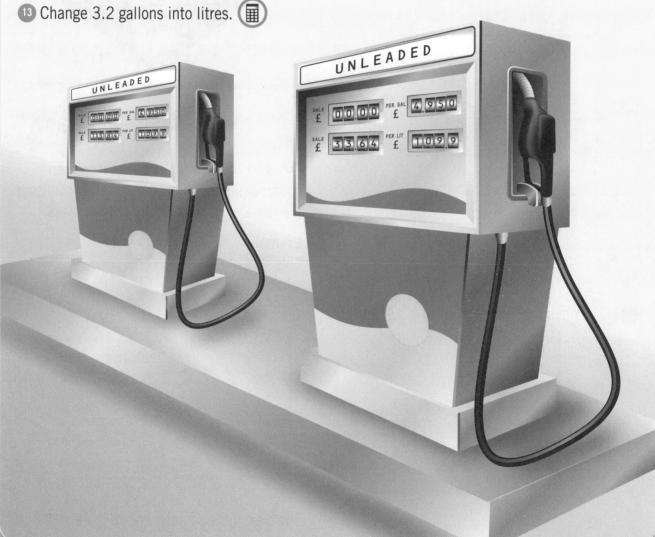

Perimeter, Area and Volume

Perimeter

The distance around the outside edge of a shape is called the **perimeter**.

For example, if you were erecting a fence in your garden, you would need to find the distance around the edge of the garden in order to know how many fence panels to buy.

Examples

The following shapes are drawn on cm^2 paper. Find the perimeter of each shape.

1

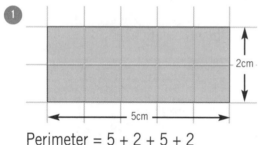

Perimeter = 5 + 2 + 5 + 2
= 14cm

2

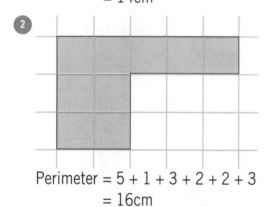

Perimeter = 5 + 1 + 3 + 2 + 2 + 3
= 16cm

3

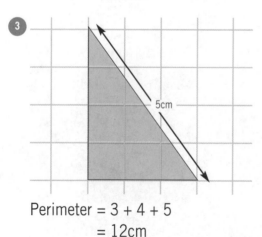

Perimeter = 3 + 4 + 5
= 12cm

Area

The **area** of a 2-D shape is the amount of space it covers.

Units of area include mm^2, cm^2 and m^2.

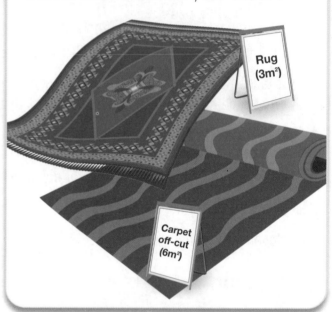

Rug
(3m^2)

Carpet
off-cut
(6m^2)

Area of an Irregular Shape

The area of an irregular shape drawn on squared paper can be estimated by counting the number of squares the shape covers.

Example

This shape is drawn on cm^2 paper. What is its area?

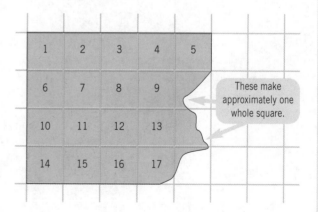

These make approximately one whole square.

The area of the shape is approximately 18cm^2.

Area of a Rectangle

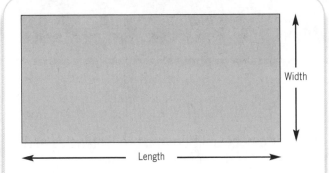

For any rectangle:

Area	=	Length	×	Width

This can be written as:

$$A = l \times w$$

Examples
Find the area of the following:

1

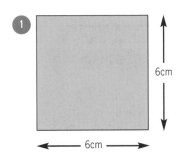

6cm

6cm

Area = $l \times w$
    = 6 × 6   ← A square has all lengths equal.
    = 36cm^2

2

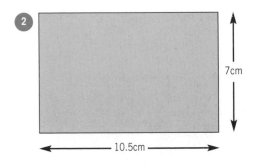

7cm

10.5cm

Area = $l \times w$
    = 10.5 × 7   Remember the units
    = 73.5cm^2 are squared.

Area of a Triangle

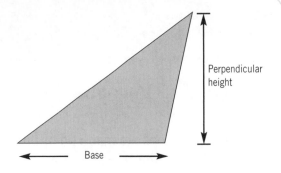

The area of a triangle is:

Area	=	$\frac{1}{2}$	×	Base	×	Perpendicular height

This can be written as:

$$A = \tfrac{1}{2} \times b \times h$$

Examples
Find the area of each of these triangles:

1

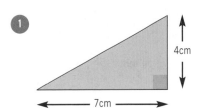

4cm

7cm

Area = $\frac{1}{2} \times b \times h$
    = $\frac{1}{2} \times 7 \times 4$
    = 14cm^2

2

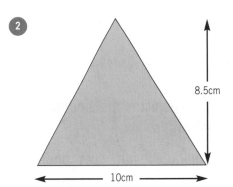

8.5cm

10cm

Area = $\frac{1}{2} \times b \times h$
    = $\frac{1}{2} \times 10 \times 8.5$
    = 42.5cm^2

Perimeter, Area and Volume

Area of a Compound Shape

Quite often, shapes are made up of different-sized rectangles and triangles. These are called compound shapes.

The area of a compound shape can be worked out in parts.

Example

Jonathan wants to tile his bathroom floor. Work out the area of the floor.

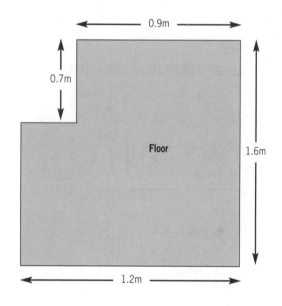

The floor can be split up into two rectangles and the area of each rectangle can be worked out.

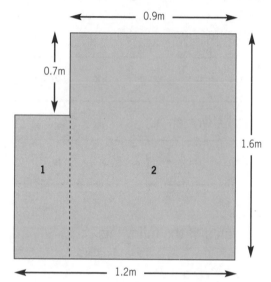

For rectangle 1, new lengths have to be calculated.

Area of rectangle 1: $A = l \times w$
$$= 0.3 \times 0.9 = 0.27m^2$$

1.2 − 0.9 = 0.3m   1.6 − 0.7 = 0.9m

Area of rectangle 2: $A = l \times w$
$$= 0.9 \times 1.6 = 1.44m^2$$

Total area $= 1.44 + 0.27$
$$= 1.71m^2$$

Volume of 3-D Solids

The **volume** of an object is the amount of space it occupies.

Units of volume include mm^3, cm^3 and m^3.

The volume of a 3-D solid can be found by counting the number of $1cm^3$ cubes it can hold.

For example, the solid opposite is made up of 9 cubes, so its volume is $9cm^3$.

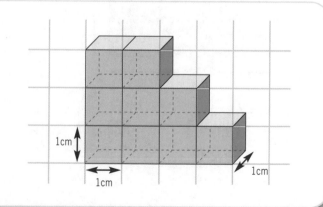

Volume of a Cuboid

A **cuboid** is a solid with rectangular faces.

Example
Work out the volume of this cuboid.

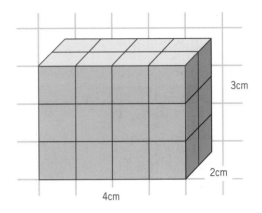

By counting cubes: Volume = 24cm³

Alternatively:

Volume of a cuboid	=	Length	×	Width	×	Height

This can be written as:

V	=	l	×	w	×	h

Example
Work out the volume of this empty box.

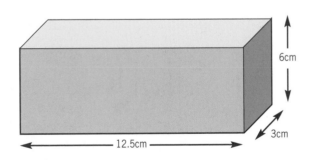

Volume = $l \times w \times h$
$$= 12.5 \times 3 \times 6$$
$$= 225\text{cm}^3$$

Quick Test

1. Explain what is meant by the perimeter of a shape.
2. A rectangle has an area of 20cm².
   If the width is 2cm what is the length?
   A 10cm
   B 20cm
   C 18cm
   D 5cm
3. What is the area of this triangle?

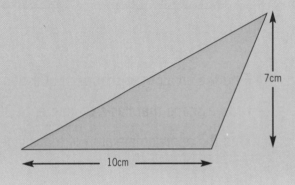

   A 70cm²
   B 140cm²
   C 35cm²
   D 35cm
4. cm² is a unit of volume. True or false?
5. The length of a cuboid is 6cm, its height is 2cm and its width is 3cm.
   What is the volume of the cuboid?
   A 11cm³
   B 15cm³
   C 30cm³
   D 36cm³

KEY WORDS
Make sure you understand these words before moving on!
- Perimeter
- Area
- Volume
- Cuboid

Perimeter, Area and Volume

Skills Practice

1 Find the perimeter of each of the following shapes drawn on cm squared paper:

a)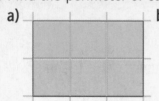

b)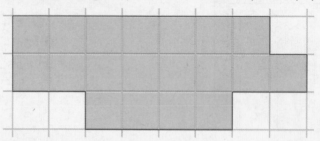

2 Find the area of the shapes in question 1 by counting squares.

3 Draw a shape that has a perimeter of 20cm.

4 Find the approximate area of this shape drawn on cm squared paper:

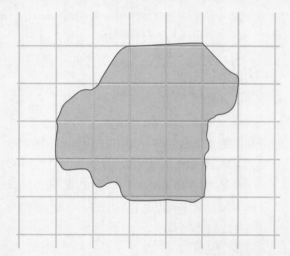

5 Find the area of each of these rectangles: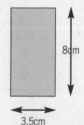

a)

2cm
6cm

c)
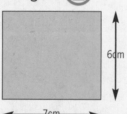
6cm
7cm

e)
8cm
3.5cm

b)
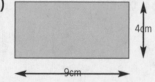
4cm
9cm

d)
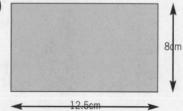
8cm
12.5cm

f)
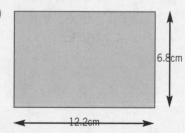
6.8cm
12.2cm

6 A rectangular picture frame measures 36cm by 42cm.
Work out...
a) the perimeter of the picture frame
b) the area of the picture frame.

7 Find the area of each of these triangles: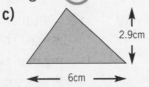

a)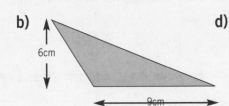

c)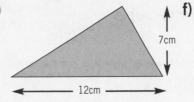

e)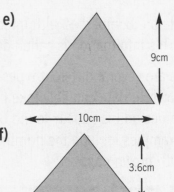

b)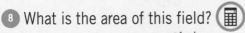

d)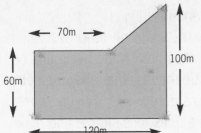

f)

8 What is the area of this field?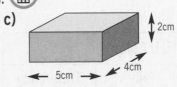

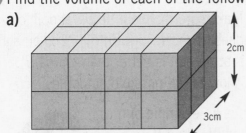

9 Find the volume of each of the following boxes:

a)

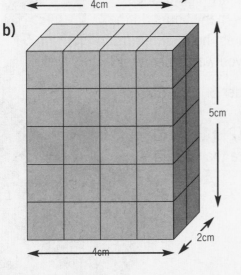

b)

c)

d)

e)

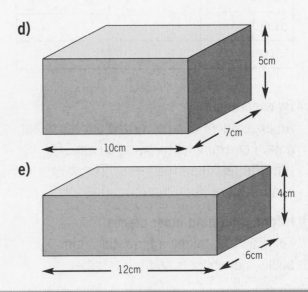

Handling Data

Data

People are bombarded with information every day. This information is called **data**.

There are several different types of data:

- **Discrete data** can only take particular values and is usually found by counting. Examples include the number of people with brown hair.

- **Continuous data** can take any value in a range. This data is often found by measuring, for example, heights of people.
- **Primary data** is data that you collect yourself.
- **Secondary data** is data that somebody else has collected.

Collecting Data

Data can be collected in several ways:

1 By observation

An observation sheet (sometimes known as a data collection sheet) can be used.

For example, an observation sheet to test the hypothesis, 'Most students have brown hair' might look like this:

Hair Colour		
Colour	Tally	Frequency
Brown		
Black		
Blonde		
Ginger		

2 By experiment

An experiment can be carried out to collect data. For example, throwing a coin 100 times to test the hypothesis, 'Throwing a head is more likely than throwing a tail'.

3 Information from other places

For example, taking information from books, newspapers and the Internet.

4 By questionnaire

Questionnaires are often used by market research companies. When designing or using questionnaires, the following points must be considered:

- Keep the questions simple and make sure that they cover the purpose of the survey.
- Make sure that your personal opinion doesn't show, for example, 'Do you agree that netball is better than football?'.
- Allow for all possible outcomes.

This is an example of a well-written question: How many hours, to the nearest hour, of television do you watch per week?

Under 3 ☐
3–7 ☐
8–12 ☐
More than 12 ☐

Organising Data

Data that's been collected can be sorted by putting it into a table called a **tally chart** or a **frequency table**. For example…

Colour of Car	Tally	Frequency
Silver	卌 卌 III	13
Red	卌 II	7
Black	II	2
Other	卌 卌	10

A tally is a mark: I.

Marks are grouped into fives to make them easy to count. The fifth mark forms a gate: 卌.

When data cover a large range of results, it's usual to group them into **class intervals**. Usually, the class intervals are the same width.

For example, in a test out of 30, the scores might be grouped as:

1–5, 6–10, 11–15, 16–20, 21–25, 26–30

A frequency table for this test might look like this:

Score	Frequency
1–5	0
6–10	6
11–15	4
16–20	10
21–25	7
26–30	3

Once the data has been sorted, it can be shown in several different types of diagram.

Pictograms

Pictograms use identical symbols, where each symbol represents a certain number of items.

Example

Number of Pizzas Sold

Ham	🍕 🍕 🍕
Cheese	🍕 🍕 ◗
Vegetarian	🍕 ◝

Key:

 = 4 pizzas

5 vegetarian pizzas were sold.

Bar Charts

Bar charts have bars of equal width to represent the frequency of discrete data.

Example

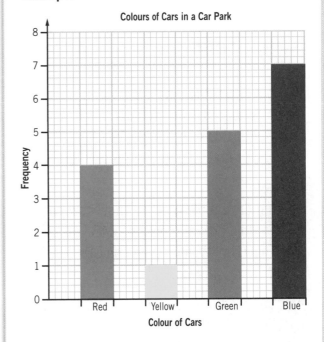

7 cars in the car park are blue.

Handling Data

Bar Line Graphs

Bar line graphs are similar to bar charts, except they use lines instead of bars to represent data.

Example

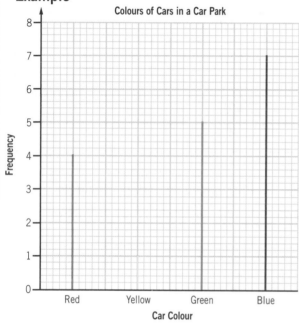

Colours of Cars in a Car Park

7 cars in the car park are blue.

Pie Charts

In a **pie chart**, the data is shown in a circle, which is split up into sections. Each section represents a certain number of items.
You need to be able to interpret pie charts.

Example

William drew a pie chart to show how he spent his monthly pocket money of £48.
How much did William spend on CDs and DVDs? (360° represents £48)

Amount spent on CDs and DVDs is represented by 150° (360° − 120° − 90° = 150°).
$$\frac{150°}{360°} \times £48 = £20$$

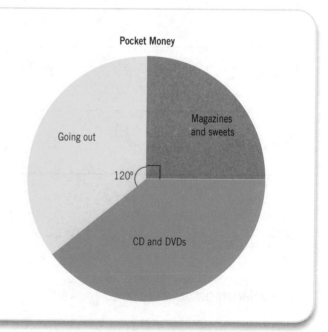

Pocket Money

Line Graphs

A **line graph** is a set of points joined by lines.

Line graphs can be used to show…
* continuous data
* how a quantity changes over time.

Example

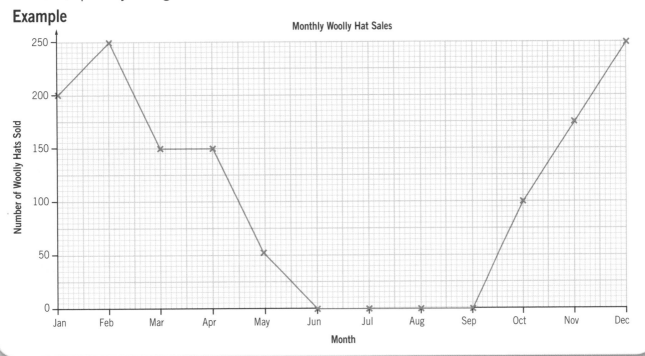

Quick Test

1. Vinay wants to find out how many pets each of his classmates has.
   a) What would be an appropriate way to collect this data?
   b) Will his data be primary or secondary?
   c) Will his data be discrete or continuous?
   d) What would be the best way of organising his data? Explain your answer.
   e) Name one method he could use to display the data.

2. What is the difference between a tally chart and a frequency table?

3. The line graph opposite shows the number of greeting cards sold by a newsagent over a year.
   a) Explain what happens to the sale of cards during the year.
   b) Why do you think sales rose in specific months?

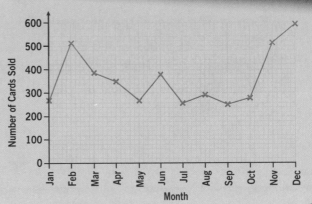

Handling Data

1. Hattie is doing a survey on the types of books people like to read.
   Design a data collection sheet that Hattie could use.

2. Ahmed included this question on his questionnaire:

   How much pocket money do you receive per week?

   £1 or less ☐

   £1 – £3 ☐

   Over £3 ☐

   Explain what is wrong with Ahmed's question.

3. A leisure centre asked 20 people what sport
   they had come to do. The answers were as follows:

Swimming	Yoga	Badminton	Squash	Yoga
Squash	Swimming	Swimming	Squash	Squash
Badminton	Yoga	Badminton	Swimming	Swimming
Yoga	Yoga	Yoga	Swimming	Squash

   a) Copy and complete the tally chart below:

Sport	Tally	Frequency
Swimming		
Squash		
Badminton		
Yoga		

   b) Draw a pictogram of the information.
   c) Copy the axes opposite and draw a
      bar chart of the leisure centre data.
   d) Which sports are the most popular at
      the leisure centre?

   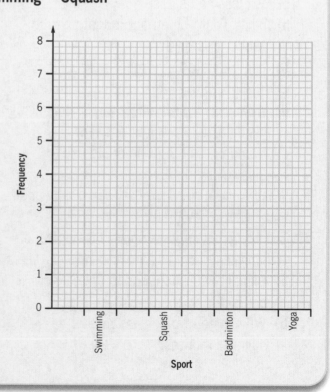

4 The bar line graph opposite shows the sales of hot drinks in a café in one day.

a) Which drink sold the most?

b) How many hot drinks were sold in total?

c) Explain why the sales of soup might have been so low.

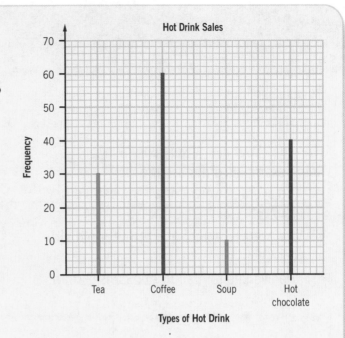

Hot Drink Sales

Frequency

Types of Hot Drink

5 Using a survey, Erin decided to find out what method of transport the students in her class had used to get to school that morning. Her findings are shown in the pie chart. There are 24 students in Erin's class.

a) How many students walked to school?

b) How many students came to school by car?

c) Give a possible reason why so few students came to school by car.

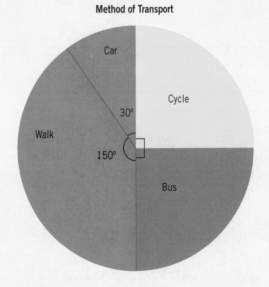

Method of Transport

Car

Cycle

30°

Walk

150°

Bus

6 The line graph shows the number of cups of tea sold in a café during a week.

a) Give possible reasons why only five cups of tea were sold on Wednesday.

b) Give possible reasons why 40 cups of tea were sold on Saturday.

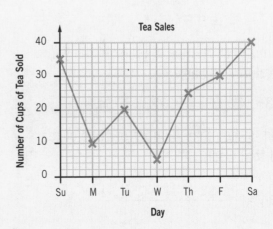

Tea Sales

Number of Cups of Tea Sold

Su   M   Tu   W   Th   F   Sa

Day

Averages

Averages

The word 'average' is very common. Some examples of its use are...

- 'the average weight of a ten-year-old boy is 47kg'
- 'the average height of a ten-year-old girl is 120cm'
- 'the average rainfall in August is 22mm'.

The average is the best representation of a set of data.

There are three different types of average that you can find for a set of data:

- the **mean**
- the **mode**
- the **median**.

Mean

The mean is one of the most commonly used averages.

$$\text{Mean} = \frac{\text{Sum of a set of values}}{\text{Number of values used}}$$

Examples

1. Lottie got the following marks in ten mental arithmetic tests:

   12, 15, 6, 9, 12, 11, 10, 9, 9, 5

   What is Lottie's mean mark?

   $\text{Mean} = \frac{12 + 15 + 6 + 9 + 12 + 11 + 10 + 9 + 9 + 5}{10}$

   $= \frac{98}{10} = 9.8$

2. The number of cups of tea sold daily in a café during a week are:

   36, 42, 31, 49, 28, 48, 54

   What is the mean number of cups of tea sold that week?

   $\text{Mean} = \frac{36 + 42 + 31 + 49 + 28 + 48 + 54}{7}$

   $= \frac{288}{7} = 41.1 \text{ (to 1 d.p.)}$

Mode

In any set of data, the mode is the value that occurs most often.

Example

The number of matches in ten matchboxes is counted. The results are as follows:

   37, 41, 37, 36, 38, 38, 39, 40, 40, 40

What is the mode of this data?

Since three boxes contain 40 matches, the mode is 40.

You can say that the 'modal number' of matches is 40.

Example

What is the mode of this data?

   6, 9, 4, 3, 6, 6, 5, 3, 7, 3, 6, 3

There are two modes: 3 and 6. This is known as **bimodal**.

Median

The median of a set of data is the middle value when the data is put in order of size.

Examples

1 The number of goals scored by a football team in their first nine matches of the season is:

3, 2, 1, 3, 4, 2, 1, 2, 3

What is the median number of goals scored?

First, arrange the data in order of size:

1, 1, 2, 2, 2, 3, 3, 3, 4

Cross off numbers from both ends to locate the middle value:

X ,X ,X ,X ,②,X ,X ,X ,X

So, the median is 2 goals.

2 Molly wants to find the median weight, to the nearest kg, of the girls in her dance group. Their weights, in kg, are:

48, 52, 47, 46, 52, 55, 53, 49, 50, 47

Find the median weight.

First, arrange the data in order of size:

46, 47, 47, 48, 49, 50, 52, 52, 53, 55

Next, locate the middle value(s):

46, 47, 47, 48, (49, 50), 52, 52, 53, 55

Since there are two values in the middle, you need to find the midpoint of these:

$$\frac{49 + 50}{2} = 49.5$$

Median weight = 49.5kg

Range

The **range** of a set of data tells you how 'spread out' the data is.

It's the difference between the highest and lowest values.

Range	=	Highest value	−	Lowest value

Example

The data shows the rainfall, in mm, of the twelve months in one year.

161, 172, 165, 152, 112, 110, 92, 27, 31, 87, 136, 141

What is the range of this data?

Range = 172 − 27 = 145mm

Making Comparisons

The average and range can be used to compare two or more sets of data.

Example

Two brands of batteries are compared. The results are shown in the table.

Brand	Mean (hours)	Range (hours)
Best Buy	16.3	5.8
Durable	16.2	1.2

Which brand represents the best value?

From the information in the table, you can see that 'Durable' is the better-value brand.

Although the average number of hours that 'Durable' batteries last for is slightly less than 'Best Buy' batteries, their range is much smaller (the spread is lower), which means that 'Durable' batteries are more reliable.

Averages

Averages from a Frequency Table

Data is often shown in **frequency tables**.

Frequency tables can be used to find the mean, median, mode and range of data.

Example
The frequency table shows the number of televisions the students of Class 7K have at home.

Number of Televisions	Frequency
0	1
1	5
2	7
3	8
4	4

Find the mean, median, mode and range of this set of data.

The table shows...
- 1 student has 0 televisions
- 5 students have 1 television
- 7 students have 2 televisions, and so on.

$$\text{Mean} = \frac{\text{Total (Frequency} \times \text{Number of televisions)}}{\text{Total of the frequency}}$$

$$= \frac{(1 \times 0) + (5 \times 1) + (7 \times 2) + (8 \times 3) + (4 \times 4)}{1 + 5 + 7 + 8 + 4}$$

$$= \frac{59}{25} = 2.36 \text{ televisions}$$

Median: Since there are 25 students, the median must be the 13th student. Counting up the frequency table gives the 13th value as 2 televisions.

Mode: This is the number of televisions with the highest frequency. The modal number of televisions is 3.

Range = Highest number of televisions –
　　　　Lowest number of televisions
　　 = 4 – 0 = 4 televisions

Quick Test

1. Explain how you would find the mode of a set of data.
2. The mode of 8, 9, 4, 8, 7, 3, 8, 7 is 7. True or false?
3. What is the range of these numbers?
   7, 9, 15, 2, 6, 3, 13
   A 9　**B** 13　**C** 2 – 15　**D** 17
4. What is the median of these numbers?
   7, 2, 9, 3, 4, 4, 6
   A 9　**B** 3　**C** 4　**D** 6
5. Explain how you would find the mean of a set of data.

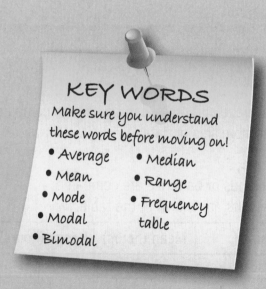

KEY WORDS
Make sure you understand these words before moving on!
- Average
- Mean
- Mode
- Modal
- Bimodal
- Median
- Range
- Frequency table

Skills Practice

1. For this set of data:
   3, 7, 9, 6, 7, 7, 4, 8, 5
   find the...
   a) mean
   b) median
   c) mode
   d) range.

2. For this set of data:
   7, 4, 9, 11, 3, 3, 8, 3
   find the...
   a) mean
   b) median
   c) mode
   d) range.

3. For this set of data:
   2.6, 4.8, 4.7, 5.2, 9.3, 4.7, 4.8, 4.7, 5.1, 4.7
   find the...
   a) mean
   b) median
   c) mode
   d) range.

4. Class 7M got a mean score of 63% in a maths test.
   The top mark was 100% and the lowest mark was 14%.

   Class 7K got a mean score of 82% in the same maths test.
   The top mark was 92% and the lowest mark was 71%.

   Which class performed the best? Explain your answer.

5. The table shows the number of experiments carried out by some students.

Number of Experiments	0	1	2	3	4
Frequency	2	7	12	20	4

   Find the mean number of experiments carried out.
   Give your answer correct to one decimal place.

6. The number of goals scored by teams in a local football league one week is shown in the table.

Number of Goals	0	1	2	3
Frequency	5	7	6	2

   a) Work out the mean number of goals scored.
   b) Work out the modal number of goals scored.
   c) Find the range of this data.

Probability

Probability

Probability is the chance or likelihood that something will happen.

The idea of chance comes up every day. For example...
- the chance of winning the lottery
- the likelihood that it'll snow on Christmas Day.

When you talk about probability, you might use words such as...
- likely
- unlikely
- evens / even chance
- impossible
- certain.

This probability line shows where each of the words comes on a scale from 'impossible' to 'certain'.

Impossible   Very unlikely   Unlikely   Even chance   Likely   Very likely   Certain

For example, a bag contains three green beads and one red bead. If a bead is taken out of the bag at random, the chance of it being green is likely and the chance of it being red is unlikely.

An event is something that happens. Every event has a set of possible outcomes. In probability, events are considered that have one or more possible outcomes.

For example, the possible outcomes when a fair dice is thrown are 1, 2, 3, 4, 5, 6.

Expressing Probabilities

The probability that an event can happen lies between 0 and 1.

The probability scale...
* starts at 0 for something that's impossible
* finishes at 1 for something that's certain.

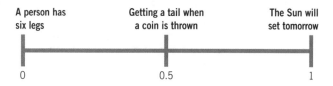

Probabilities can be written as...
* fractions
* decimals
* percentages

Never write probabilities using the words 'out of'.

Example

A bag contains five red counters, one blue counter and four yellow counters.
A counter is chosen at random.
On a probability scale...

a) mark with an R the probability of choosing a red counter
b) mark with a B the probability of choosing a blue counter
c) mark with a G the probability of choosing a green counter.

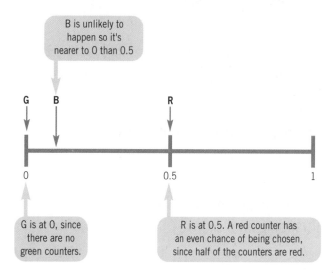

B is unlikely to happen so it's nearer to 0 than 0.5

G is at 0, since there are no green counters.

R is at 0.5. A red counter has an even chance of being chosen, since half of the counters are red.

Calculating Probabilities

Probabilities can be calculated by...
* doing experiments
* using theory
* collecting data.

If you know what all the possible outcomes of an event are, you can calculate the probability of something happening:

Probability of an outcome	=	Number of ways an outcome can happen / Total number of outcomes

P(outcome) is the shortened way of writing the probability of an outcome.

The total of the probabilities for all possible outcomes of an event is 1.

Example

The letters that spell out the word 'trigonometry' are placed in a container.
A letter is taken out at random.
What is the probability of taking out...

a) a letter T?
$$P(T) = \frac{2}{12} = \frac{1}{6}$$

b) a vowel?
$$P(vowel) = \frac{4}{12} = \frac{1}{3}$$

c) a letter A?
$$P(A) = 0$$
Since there's no letter A, the probability is zero.

Probability

Experimental Probability

Sometimes an experiment is carried out to show all the possible outcomes of an event, before estimating probabilities of particular outcomes.

For example, Samuel threw a fair dice 60 times to estimate the probability of getting a six. Here are his results:

Six	Not six
13	47

There are 60 possible outcomes of which 13 are favourable so...
P(landing on a six) = $\frac{13}{60}$

Theoretically, you would expect...
P(landing on a six) = $\frac{10}{60}$

It's unlikely if Samuel was to repeat the experiment that he would get exactly the same result, but he will get a score similar to $\frac{10}{60}$.

Quick Test

1. Explain what probability is.
2. A bag contains three red beads and two green beads.
   A bead is taken out of the bag at random.
   What is the probability that it's...
   a) red?
      A $\frac{2}{5}$ B 1 C $\frac{3}{5}$ D 0
   b) green?
      A $\frac{2}{5}$ B 1 C $\frac{3}{5}$ D 0
   c) red or green?
      A $\frac{2}{5}$ B 1 C $\frac{3}{5}$ D 0
3. The number of outcomes when a fair dice is thrown is 6. True or false?
4. The probability of getting a head on a fair coin is $\frac{1}{2}$. True or false?

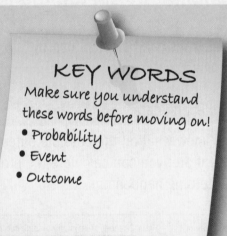

KEY WORDS
Make sure you understand these words before moving on!
• Probability
• Event
• Outcome

1 Write down whether each of the following outcomes is 'certain', 'impossible' or 'possible':
a) You'll throw a 9 with a regular dice.
b) You'll have a birthday on the same date each year.
c) Your friend will go to Mars next summer.
d) You'll receive an email from a friend tonight.

2 Copy the likelihood scale below.

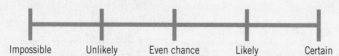

Impossible   Unlikely   Even chance   Likely   Certain

Mark each of these outcomes on the scale.
a) It'll rain in Manchester next year.
b) The next baby born will be female.
c) You'll live until you're 300 years old.
d) The next person you'll see is famous.

3 A, B, C and D are four outcomes that have been marked on this probability scale:

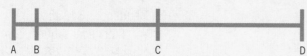

A   B   C   D

Write down possible outcomes that A, B, C and D could be.

4 List all possible outcomes for each of the following events:
a) Spinning this spinner.
b) Picking a counter from this box without looking.

5 A bag contains three red, four blue and two green counters.
A counter is taken from the bag at random.
What is the probability that the chosen counter is...
a) red?
b) yellow?
c) blue?

6 A multipack of crisps contains two cheese and onion, four ready salted, four salt and vinegar and one smoky bacon.
Thomas takes a bag of crisps without looking at the flavours.
What is the probability that Thomas picks...
a) cheese and onion?
b) ready salted?
c) smoky bacon?
d) prawn cocktail?

Activity

Throw a coin 200 times. Record your results in a tally chart.

Work out the experimental probability of the coin landing on tails.

$$\text{Experimental probability of landing on tails} = \frac{\text{Number of times your coin landed on tails}}{\text{Total number of times you threw the coin}}$$

Compare the theoretical probability with the experimental probability.

Index